THE MAKING OF A MASTERPIECE

The Fowokan George Kelly Story

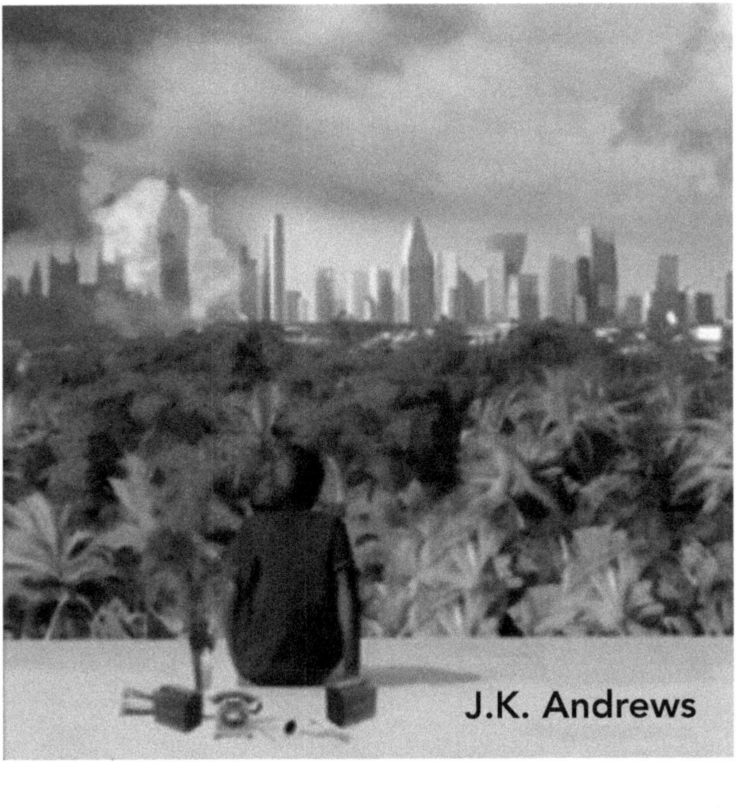

Conscious Dreams
PUBLISHING

The Making of a Masterpiece: The Fowokan George Kelly Story

I have tried to recreate events, locales and conversations from my memories of them. In order to maintain their anonymity in some instances I have changed the names of individuals and places, I may have changed some identifying characteristics and details such as physical properties, occupations and places of residence.

Published by Conscious Dreams Publishing
www.consciousdreamspublishing.com

Edited by Elise Abram
Typeset and E-book formatting by Amit Dey
Cover Design by @carriacou_designs

ISBN: 978-1-917584-40-1

ACKNOWLEDGMENTS

Thanks to Richard Liston, Cathy Rosario, Laura Yeates, Byron Lye-Fook, Tulla Seddon, Sandra Roberts, Merline Grant, Margaret Andrews and Ronald Hermann.

Special thanks to Hassan Aliyu for providing the image for the sculpture 'Meditations Beneath Duppy Cherry Tree'.

Finally, thanks to Fowokan for bestowing me the honour of capturing your history in this body of work.

Fowokan, I do hope it does you the justice you truly deserve!

CONTENTS

INTRODUCTION

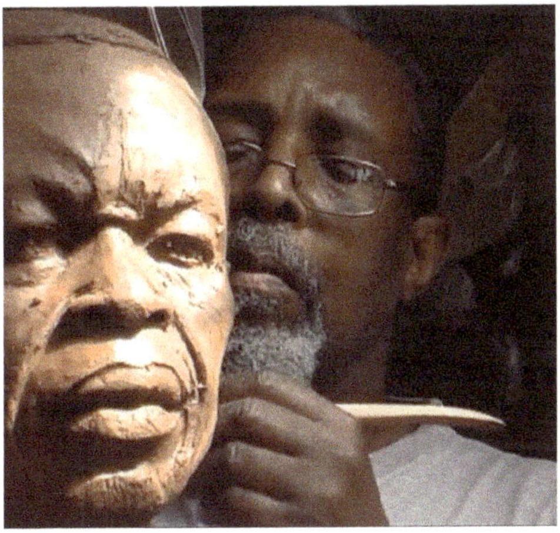

This book is about the life of Fowokan George Kelly as he navigates his journey from being a curious and creative boy to becoming a well-known and respected artist. I've captured his life story from the many memorable conversations at his home and retold them in a manner that I hope evokes the feelings and emotions of certain characters. I have altered some names and a few physical and geographical features to preserve individuals' privacy.

THE BEGINNING, WHERE IT ALL BEGAN

In Kingston, the capital of Jamaica, Lona and Eubert Kelly welcomed their first son into the world: George Kelly. He grew up to become a successful contemporary creative artist and would go on to spend most of his life in the United Kingdom.

George was inspired by African art and produced amazing 3D models despite having no prior knowledge or training in art or history.

He travelled to many countries and enjoyed learning about their uniquely different cultures and traditions. However, there was one country that changed the course of his destiny.

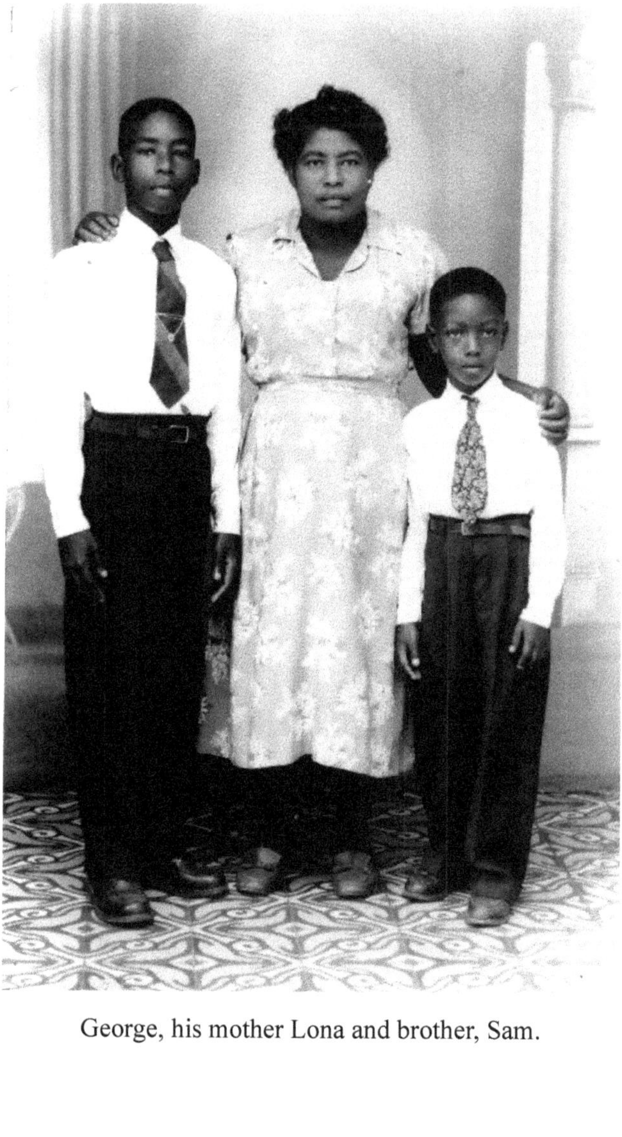

George, his mother Lona and brother, Sam.

GEORGE, THE EARLY YEARS

As a young boy growing up in Jamaica, all his friends and neighbours were sure that George would grow up and work in a technical field such as engineering. He could turn his hand to many things, often beyond the limits of his age. However, destiny had other ideas for this remarkably creative boy.

Kenness George Kelly was born on 1 April 1943 in Jubilee Hospital, Kingston, Jamaica. As a result of people mispronouncing his first name, he chose to use his middle name.

George started school at three years old. In those days, writing was completed on slate boards using a slate pencil, adding to the fun of learning. He then went on to attend Calabar Elementary School, also known as East Queen Street Baptist Elementary School, when he was five years old. This was when he began using exercise books. However, before learning the alphabet, he was taught to shape clay into tiny figures resembling little Buddhas. Learning was done mainly through play, with teachers encouraging discovery and creativity.

Upon entering elementary school, he quickly became an eager student, learning how to read and write as well as how to make models and toys. George enjoyed most lessons at school and excelled at creative subjects.

After school, George and his friends would play outside, making toys using the skills they learnt in class. They also enjoyed exploring the neighbourhood and getting up to mischief!

Creating art was always a part of George's life. It was not uncommon for children in Jamaica to make skates (a version of a bicycle), dolls, miniature boats to race, kites, slingshots (catapults), gigs (spinning tops) and a variety of objects out of cedar wood and clay.

The clay, which naturally occurs in the south of the island of Jamaica, was used to make bricks and clay pots called Yabba. There was also an abundance of cedar trees where George lived, which had a pleasant aroma. This was the wood that local factories used for making cigar boxes. George and his friends would go to the wood-cutting factory and collect the off-cuts to make dolls for girls in the community. The softness of the wood made it easy for the boys to carve using their only tool: a penknife. The coarse fibres or cords from large calico bags, which stored flour, were used to make their hair. The boys would give the dolls to the girls they liked most and even to the girls they did not like.

Children regularly saw painters at work when the newest movies were shown at the many open-air cinemas in Kingston. Skilled painters designed posters by creating scenes featuring characters from the latest upcoming films, often completing them in a single day! There were many different film genres, but Westerns and gangster films were George's and his friends' favourites.

People would stop and watch admiringly as the artists stood on scaffolding, painting on the giant billboards outside the cinemas. They watched as the artists drew outlines and applied vibrant colours and textures to bring them to life. Observing this amazing creativity, bringing characters and scenes to life, was an important early experience for George. Competitions arose between the boys in his neighbourhood as to who could draw the best portrait of a cowboy, as featured in American comic books and films.

As George grew older, he sought other ways to occupy his time. In Jamaica in the 1950s, very few houses had the luxury of electric lighting, but the ever-resourceful George knew how to create electricity. He would go down to the British Army Dump where the military disposed of used dry cell batteries, collect them, and take them home. George then linked them in series with copper wire he took from old electric motors and attached them to a light bulb in the house. Attaching bulbs and metal produced enough electricity to light the interior and exterior of his family's home.

He was very community-minded, though, and being a natural leader, he passed on his knowledge of how to do this by teaching other young boys in the neighbourhood.

Having created electricity to light up homes, he thought it would be a clever idea to have a telephone in his house, but there was only one problem: his parents could not afford a phone. However, this little technicality did not deter George. He used old scrapped telephones from the nearby dump to create his own system, thus allowing him to communicate with his neighbours. He did all of this by the age of twelve.

George emerged as an incredibly talented boy. It was no surprise that his friends and their parents believed he would become an engineer.

Another pastime George enjoyed as a young boy was standing at the foot of Wareika Hill, looking towards Palisadoes Airport in Kingston, which was later renamed Norman Manley International Airport. He would watch planes land and take off, wondering what it would be like to be on board one of those amazing machines. He loved seeing the planes grow smaller and smaller as they soared higher and higher into the brilliant blue sky before they disappeared out of sight. George imagined himself on one of the aeroplanes going to America and being a cowboy, slaying all the bad guys just like in the movies.

Westerns and gangster movies were so popular in Jamaica that they generated a huge fascination with the American way of life. It was the place George and most of his friends dreamt of visiting. He hoped that one day, he would have the opportunity to visit the States.

OUT OF MANY, ONE PEOPLE

George's parents, Lona and Eubert, were loving but strict. They passed on their wisdom and knowledge through a mixture of riddles, proverbs and Anansi stories from the Ashanti people of Ghana. The main character was a wily, cunning spider called Anansi, who was a trickster. The stories always had a moral tale to guide and direct young and old alike.

Now and then, come evening, George's parents built a fire, and family and neighbours gathered around the flickering flames and waited for the entertainment to begin. In those days, there were no television broadcasts in Jamaica, but that did not seem to matter. Some locals were expert storytellers and had everyone spellbound, entertaining the community with tales of Anansi and *duppy* (ghost) stories.

George's parents lived through the awful effects of the October 1929 Wall Street Crash in the U.S.A. and the poverty of the 1930s. The stock market crash marked the beginning of a decade of depression that made life extremely difficult for people around the world, including Jamaica, and many villagers were forced to migrate from the countryside to find a better standard of living. Lona and Eubert were no exception. They settled in Downtown Kingston.

The island's capital was a place of constant change. Once villagers moved to Kingston, they worked hard until they could afford to move to more affluent neighbourhoods.

Eventually, some professional workers migrated to the U.S.A. and Canada. Jamaican nurses, who were trained under the British educational system, were well regarded and highly sought after. Others, who did not have professional jobs, travelled as contract workers to labour chopping sugar cane in Cuba or as orange pickers in Florida. There was a tradition of migrating to find work, such as those who left Jamaica to help with the construction of the Panama Canal. However, some of them never returned. You can still find communities of the descendants of Jamaicans today in Cuba and Panama.

The enormous loss of lives on the battlefields during the Second World War, along with the destruction of cities and towns due to the frequent bombing, meant there was a shortage of labour to rebuild Britain. From the late 1940s, Britain advertised for workers from its colonies to help reconstruct their devastated country.

On 22 June 1948, the SS *Empire Windrush*, a troop ship carrying 1,027 people from the Caribbean Islands, of which 492 were Jamaicans, arrived at Tilbury Docks. The passengers were mainly ex-servicemen who had fought in World War Two and were returning to Britain. On board, there were also two Jamaican women who were nurses.

British Caribbean people who arrived from 1948 to 1971 are now known as the Windrush Generation. Under the colonial system, West Indians were born British, but this did not give them automatic rights to migrate to the United Kingdom. All of this changed after the introduction of the

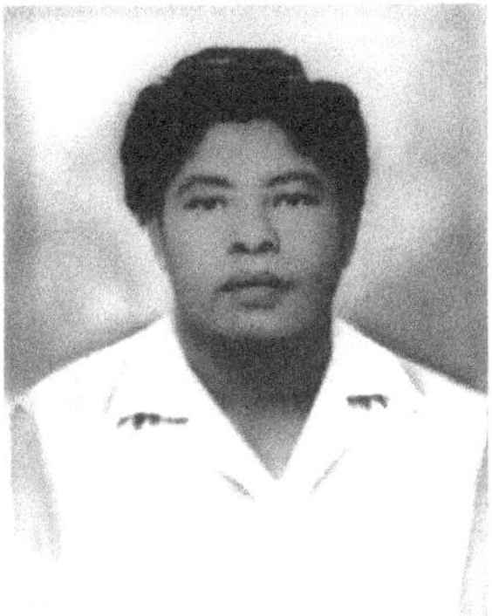

1948 Nationality Act when people from the colonies were allowed to settle in the U.K. George's parents, along with thousands of other Caribbean people, felt the pull towards the 'Mother Country', due to the shortage of workers in the transport system, General Post Office, NHS, as well as unskilled workers, such as labourers.

George's Mother, Lona Cherry Gibbs, was born on 19 March 1920 and was named by her father. She came from the parish of St Ann in a village called Content. Lona is Yoruba for 'the one who comes to prepare the way'. She had two siblings: Edland, the eldest, and Lynette, the youngest. She moved to Kingston, Jamaica, when she was eight.

After the abolition of slavery, Lona's great-grandparents, Mr. and Mrs. Williams, were a white Welsh couple who inherited a small plantation in Content. This was common after slavery ended, as many Irish, Scottish and Welsh families inherited plantations once worked by enslaved people. Over time, their descendants became darker as they formed relationships with the local population. On George's paternal side, his European heritage was Irish, with the surname Kelly passed down through that lineage. However, he was never told any stories or family history about their origins.

Mr and Mrs Williams, lived in a two-storey stone house that is still standing today. One of the descendants of the Williams family still takes care of the remains of the estate. Mr and Mrs Williams owned a shipping company used to transport merchandise between Runaway Bay and Cuba. Runaway Bay is a small coastal town in the parish of St Ann on the northern coast of Jamaica. It is said to be where the Spanish were allowed to leave the island after the British captured Jamaica from them in 1655.

Lona was a caring person who was much loved by her family and people in the community. She was particularly helpful to the elderly, often bringing them food and visiting the sick. She excelled at school and used this knowledge to help others, including those who could not read. Lona was introduced to Eubert through their families, and after a short courtship, they were married in Kingston in 1942.

George's father, Eubert Samuel James Kelly, was born in 1904 in the parish of St Ann in a village called Thicketts, which is about two miles from the village of Content. Eubert worked on his family's land instead of going to school, which meant that his reading and writing skills were limited. Eubert left Thicketts when he was probably a teenager and arrived in Downtown Kingston, where he stayed with his older sister, Charlotte. Once Eubert got married, he left Charlotte's house and set up a home with his new wife, Lona.

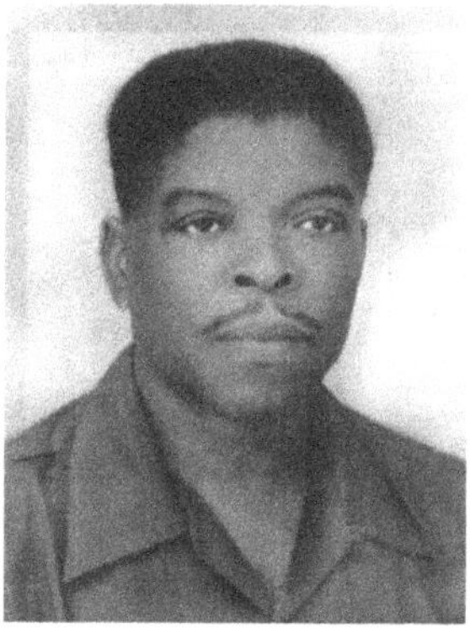

Eubert took George to spend time with his aunt Charlotte most Saturday mornings, usually after a visit to one of the outdoor cinemas to watch the silent movie of the day. Even though Eubert found some words difficult to read, he loved silent movies, especially ones starring Charlie Chaplin. Out of the eight or so cinemas in Kingston, he took his son to the cinema that only showed silent movies.

Eubert spent his early life in Kingston, taking any work he could find to provide for his young family. He moved from one job to another, even taking up professional boxing before working in a bakery owned by Chinese Jamaicans. After some time, he went on to start his own bakery, and his business flourished.

In the early 1950s, Eubert had trouble getting flour, so he sold the bakery and thought about migrating to England. With the help of his wife, Eubert applied for a British passport in 1956 to travel to Britain along with thousands of other West Indians who heeded the call to help rebuild Britain. Later that year, he left Jamaica for England while Lona and his two young sons stayed behind.

When Eubert arrived in Britain, it did not take him long to find work. His first job was working as a labourer on a building site before going on to work in a sausage factory on Albany Road, Walworth, southeast London, which has since been demolished and is now part of Burgess Park.

Eubert struggled to make friends at work and often felt lonely, as his workmates never invited him to lunch. Living with others didn't help either, as their talks about the cold weather, racism, and disrespect only made him feel worse. In the evenings, when he was alone, hearing his neighbours' cheerful voices through the walls only made him feel even more lonely.

Eubert missed his wife and family very much, but he could not afford to pay their passage because his wages were so low. Fortunately, he joined a 'pardner' with a group of Caribbean friends to save money to pay the fare for his family to join him. A pardner, also known as a 'susu' on some islands in the Eastern Caribbean, is a way of saving money in which a group of friends pays a fixed weekly sum of money to a banker. Each week, the banker gives one person the total sum collected. This is repeated weekly until all people in the pardner get their 'hand' or share. Once everyone has their hand, the cycle starts again with the same group of people or with new ones joining. After a few pardner hands, Eubert had only managed to save enough money to pay for his wife's passage to England.

Lona joined him in February 1957 and soon found work. Eubert made plans for both of them to invest some of their earnings into another pardner to send for their sons, for whom he had big plans. He wanted George and Sam to have better opportunities than he ever had. Eubert, like many Caribbean people, thought that an English education was the best one could get, and he would ensure that his sons studied hard and obtained good jobs.

Auntie Lyn

While Eubert and Lona settled in England, George and Sam, George's younger brother by seven years, were left with their aunt, Lynette Brown, Lona's younger sister. She was a wise woman, admired and respected by people in the community. At the time, Auntie Lyn had no children of her own, so she welcomed the opportunity to look after her nephews, whom she loved and cherished.

George's maternal grandfather, Esau Gibbs, went to Cuba in the 1920s and regularly posted money home to his wife. In

1929, after many years of enduring the hardships of labouring in the fields, he returned to Jamaica, where Lynette was born, thus completing their family.

Auntie Lyn was a member of a *Pocomania* church (Pocomania means 'little madness'). Their faith is a blend of African religious beliefs and Christianity. Auntie Lyn dressed in her white robe and white head tie, like all the members of the congregation. On special occasions, she took George and Sam to church with her. They were blessed by the Mother and given consecrated water to drink and wash away illnesses.

George marvelled at the way women, mainly, would 'catch the spirit' through a ritual of breathing and speaking in tongues. When they got into the spirit, the women spun around and fell to the ground. Auntie Lyn was no different. When she caught the spirit, she, too, would spin and speak in tongues before collapsing.

As lovely as it was to be in the care of their aunt, George and his brother missed their parents. Although his mother wrote letters and sent parcels of clothes and money along with promises that he and his brother would be joining them, they couldn't wait to see them. He and his brother were constantly told by their aunt, 'Dem gonna send for you soon, boys,' but soon was taking a very long time to come!

COMING TO THE MOTHER COUNTRY

Lona and Eubert settled in a four-storey house at 3, Geneva Road, Brixton, South West London, which was near to Lambeth Town Hall, with its chiming clock. Many years later, whenever George heard the sound of the Lambeth Town Hall clock chiming, it would take him back to the very first morning of his arrival in England when the sound of the clock woke him up.

Eubert and Lona slept separately. Eubert had rented a double bed in a room on the top floor. The room also contained three other single beds, occupied by six men doing shift work. Lona, meanwhile, shared a room two floors below with a close friend from Jamaica.

On the landing, there was a cooker used by around twelve tenants who lived on that floor. The house had no bathroom, just a single toilet in the basement.

At the time, many English homes, particularly those without indoor bathrooms, used the kitchen sink for washing and brushing their teeth, while a tin bath was used for bathing. Most newcomers, however, had no choice but to use a basin of water, and if they were lucky, they might have had a sink in their room.

In most London Councils there were public baths. Camberwell Green Public Baths was the nearest baths for the tenants of Geneva Road. For a small sum of money Lona, Eubert, and people in the area were able to have regular baths.

When Lona departed for England leaving George and Sam behind, she hoped that her sons would behave and not get into any trouble, but George's strong desire to listen to the radio made him do something illegal. One afternoon, he climbed the telephone pole outside the house and connected a speaker to the radio cable. Using his self-taught technical knowledge, he tapped into their radio cable to listen to music and local gossip. The radio company 'Rediffusion' detected interference, realising the lines were being used illegally and reported it to the police. Through careful monitoring and surveillance, they traced the signal to Auntie Lyn's house and went to arrest those who were responsible for the crime.

A few days later, as George and his friends were relaxing, and listening to music, a police van was quickly dispatched and noisily arrived outside Auntie Lyn's house. Wiretapping was a serious offence and if caught would lead to a prison sentence. If you were a minor, though, you were sent to a school for juvenile delinquents. When the boys saw the van , they knew what was coming. They fled, but George and a few of his friends were not as fast as the rest of the boys and were caught. Scared stiff about what was to come, George prepared himself for the worst. Luckily, at that moment, a local man he vaguely knew appeared and spoke to one of the police officers, who decided to let the boys off with a warning. George took that as a sign to change his behaviour.

At the end of August 1957, Lona and Eubert sent airline tickets for George and Sam to join them in England. By then, George was fourteen, and Sam was seven years old. George had always yearned to go on an aeroplane, never dreaming that one day he would really board one. The exhilaration of going to England to join his parents felt so overwhelming that George could not wait for the date to arrive, and he knew Sam felt the same.

George and Sam stared at the aeroplane that had bold letters—BOAC (British Overseas Airways Corporation)—painted on the side. George felt the butterflies tighten in his stomach as they approached the plane, climbed the stairs and took their seats. When the plane took off, George gazed through the window, staring at the great expanse of the Blue Mountains he was leaving behind, wondering what England would hold for him and his little brother.

George knew that he and Sam were starting a new chapter in their lives. Would they like it in England? He had heard that England was cold - would it be as cold and frosty as Newcastle, a chilly town on the Blue Mountains, where the British Army was stationed? George could not imagine anywhere as cold as Newcastle, but he was eager to find out. Well, no matter, he and Sam were prepared. Both had worn long trousers and long-sleeved shirts. In their 'grips' (which were suitcases made from cardboard), Auntie Lyn ensured they had packed a pullover and a jacket for the journey. Yes! They were both ready for cold England.

On the way to the Mother Country, the plane was scheduled to stop at Newark Airport, New Jersey, America. The boys spent two nights there while repairs to the plane were carried out. The airline company booked the passengers into a nearby hotel, and George and Sam spent some of their time in shopping malls, only returning to the hotel in the evening.

The ever-helpful and friendly airline staff acted as guides and took some of the passengers on sightseeing coach tours around the city. This gave George and Sam a real sense of what America was like. He loved America. The landscape was so different from the tropical island of Jamaica. This amazing, beautiful, concrete jungle was a stark contrast to the beaches, lush green vegetation, and mountains he was used to seeing in Jamaica. New Jersey reminded him of scenes in American gangster movies.

America was exactly how George imagined it would be. His short excursions around the city made him feel as if he were on a Hollywood film set. In Jamaica, he and his friends would climb up onto trees or high fences to watch the latest films in the open-air cinemas. As the actors shot at each other, George and his friends used their fingers to mimic guns and join in the action, firing at the screen, accompanying each shot with a shout of '*Pow*! *Pow*!' Then, he and his friends put their fingers back in their holsters (inside the waistband of their trousers), just like the cowboys and gangsters on the screen.

He marvelled at the scenery and wished he could stay a little longer. He made a promise to himself that he would return when he was older, and he did. The next time George and Sam set foot in America was in 1973 when they toured up and down the East Coast for six months; Sam was the drummer with the band Cymande, and George was their manager.

The second stop on their journey to the U.K. was in Canada at Gander Airport, Newfoundland. The plane stopped for a third time at Shannon Airport, Ireland, before arriving at London Airport on 3 September 1957. In those days, London Airport was a single building with an air traffic control tower.

Once the aeroplane doors had opened, George and Sam walked down the steps onto the tarmac. The rush of the chilly September air hit George, and he shuddered involuntarily. It was as cold as ice, and he felt the chill penetrate his whole body. It was an experience he was unprepared for, and he soon reached for his pullover and jacket.

From London Airport, George and Sam travelled by coach to Victoria Coach Station, where they were met by their parents, who each took turns hugging Sam and George. The boys were finally receiving the loving hugs from their parents they so dearly looked forward to. George couldn't help but notice that his father was a little bigger than the last time he saw him. Lona looked at each of her boys, relieved that the family was now reunited. 'Lawd, me so glad you both reach England safely. We missed you, you see. Come, we go take you to your new home. Your Pa has made you your favourite: rice and peas and chicken.' George's mouth watered at the thought. The food he ate on the aeroplane and in New Jersey was okay, but he was looking forward to the home-cooked meals he was used to.

They took a taxi to their parents' home in Brixton, which has since been demolished and is now a large council estate known as the Barrier Block. George was eager to see his new home and get some hot food. He couldn't help but notice how different New Jersey was from London. New Jersey's skies were clear, bright and sunny, whereas London's skies were grey, gloomy and cold. He also noticed the strange, thick, sooty smoke billowing from the chimneys, infiltrating the air.

The taxi stopped outside 3 Geneva Road, Brixton. George and Sam gazed up at the tall, four-storey Victorian house as it towered above them. The house had discoloured white flaking paint on each window frame. There were no nets on the windows, only brown curtains, which were drawn back to expose naked light bulbs at each window on the ground floor. Stairs went up to the front door and down to the basement. The house was bordered by black-painted iron railings, which made the huge building look foreboding and threatening. George could not help but wonder what lay behind its walls.

He became aware of his mother's arm gently ushering him into his new home, momentarily interrupting his thoughts. George and his brother followed their parents inside, and clutching his grip tightly, he climbed the stairs in trepidation. He was looking forward to living as a family again under one roof, but to his dismay, George found that his parents were not living in the same room, which felt strange to him. His mother and her friend shared a room two floors below, while his father rented a double bed in a large room on the top floor.

Sam and George looked around the room. It had sparse, basic furniture: a single wardrobe, a dressing table, a tall, blue cupboard to store food and kitchen utensils, a white enamel bucket in the corner of the room and a paraffin heater in the centre of the room. He looked down at the floor covering, which was a thin, red-brick-effect linoleum.

George's eyes were drawn to the three single beds and one double bed in the room. He wondered which bed was his and Sam's. His dad must have read his mind because he explained that the room was shared with six other men! If that was the case, George thought, where would he and Sam sleep?

His dad explained that the six men did shift work, and as they all worked different hours, they each paid the landlord to sleep in the beds at different times of the day and night, but Eubert's double bed was just for him and his sons. George felt depressed and disappointed. He discovered that out of the 25 or so male tenants who lived in the house, most of the men rented beds.

George silently hoped that his parents would move to a new house, one without the chaos of so many tenants, the inconvenience of sharing a single toilet in the basement, and the lack of privacy. The primitive living conditions were not what he and his brother were used to. In Jamaica, he and his brother had their own bedroom as well as their own toilet and shower.

He thought to himself that school would at least offer a welcome change from staying in the house. He was looking forward to starting school and could not help wondering how different an English school would be from his school in Jamaica. More importantly, he hoped to make friends.

SCHOOL

Lona had to register George and Sam with the educational authorities for them to start school, which, at the time, was located on Acre Lane, Brixton. While George, Sam and his mother were crossing the road in front of Lambeth Town Hall, a seemingly crazy old Jamaican man stopped them and shouted to Lona, 'Don mek you pickney dem talk like dem people yah!' a phrase George always remembered throughout the years. In other words, he should not become completely English but hold onto his Jamaican identity.

George started at Kennington Secondary Modern Boys' School in the 4th year (Year 10). Out of about 500 boys in the school, there were only four Black boys, which included a boy of mixed-race heritage.

On his first day, George was seated next to a Black boy who was born in England. His name was Winston Churchill Townsend. Winston was slim and handsome and stood a foot taller than most of his classmates. He was popular and well-liked amongst his peers. Winston spoke with a cockney accent, and with George's thick Kingstonian dialect, neither could understand the other.

Winston was the leader of a group of cigarette smokers, and outside of class, he avoided George at every opportunity.

George was disappointed, as although he and Winston had little in common, he liked Winston and hoped that they would become friends, but that never happened. Fortunately, friendship came to George from an unexpected source.

There was another group of boys who also stood out, a group of three boys no one could understand. They were from Glasgow and had thick Glaswegian accents. The boys were concerned that George had no friends, so they took him under their wing.

The small band of four boys became a little gang, staying together and supporting one another, especially during break times, when they might be bullied or harassed. Two of the boys George remembered were Ken Dewing and Wally McDonald. Wally McDonald was completely obsessed with his blond hair, always combing it to keep his Teddy Boy hairstyle in place.

However, George's new friends couldn't protect him from his tormentors, which meant he had to prove himself by fighting almost every day whenever he was taunted.

Another Jamaican boy, Leroy, who started on the same day as George but was a year younger, also fought every day, often several times a day! Leroy had so many fights that he passed his initiation test with flying colours, and by the summer of the following year, he was accepted and even spoke with a perfect Cockney accent, unlike George, who kept his Jamaican accent. Eventually, when the boys saw that George was no pushover and could handle himself, the daily taunts and fights gradually fizzled out.

Being at secondary school was such an adventure for George. He watched everyone, mesmerised by their different hair and eye colours. In Jamaica, most people had the same brown-coloured eyes, although there were a few whose eyes were hazel or blue. Likewise, the other pupils stared at George with mutual awe.

Their behaviour was so different from the boys in Jamaica. George was particularly struck by how some pupils misbehaved in class and were rude to the teachers. A few even dared to answer back. However, most of the teachers were strict and would never stand for rudeness or pupils talking in class, especially when the teacher was speaking.

Poor behaviour at Calabar, George's primary school in Jamaica, never happened, but if it did, the punishment would be swift, and the offending pupil would perhaps be sent to the headteacher, Mr Barrett. Once in his office, the pupil would be beaten with a cane or a thick leather strap on their bottom for a set number of lashes, depending on the offence. He would never ask the reason why the pupil had been sent to his office before administering immediate punishment. After receiving their beating, they would be sent back to class.

At Kennington Secondary Modern Boys' School, the cane was the main form of punishment. The pupil would be asked the reason why he had been sent to the headmaster, who, depending on his mood or the offence, would give the unruly child a sermon about breaking the school's rules. For minor offences, such as speaking in class, pupils would be given 50 or 100 lines while in detention. They might be told to write something like: 'I must not talk when the teacher is talking,' on separate lines multiple times. This was a boring exercise, not to mention the aching and cramping of the fingers. George studied the rule breakers and made up his mind not to misbehave in class.

During George's third art lesson, he had his first and only confrontation with a teacher. He liked art and always looked forward to his lessons. The teacher addressed the class and explained the lesson. The boys were told they had to paint a London scene, but the only time George had ever seen chimneys was on the rooftops of factories in Kingston. Seeing them in London was extremely strange and alien to him.

He collected his materials and began to paint what he knew, scenes from his memories of Jamaica, not London. He became absorbed in his painting, applying brush strokes to create vivid scenes that transported him back to these memories. Remembering the poster painter's use of vibrant colours, he added rich tones to his picture, smiling as he watched the scene come to life.

However, his thoughts were abruptly interrupted when he became aware of a dark shadow spreading slowly across his work. He looked up smiling, waiting expectantly for the teacher to praise his marvellous painting.

The art teacher gazed at his work. George thought he was pleased until he saw the teacher's face gradually become a deep shade of crimson and a scowl spread across his face. He could not understand why his teacher was so angry and the smile soon left George‘s face. Until then, George had always painted scenes that were familiar to him: steep green mountains, the sun high up in the bright blue cloudless sky, coconut trees, banana plants, and a crisp, golden, sandy beach. But his art teacher took exception to what George had painted. He'd expected George to paint what was familiar to London: grey and foggy landscapes with smoke billowing out of chimneys.

The art teacher became furious, convinced that George had intentionally ignored his instructions. He shouted in anger, and George felt a wave of intense embarrassment wash over him, but he waited patiently until the teacher had stopped shouting before calmly walking out of the class without saying a word. He did not attend another art lesson. That was the end of art for George at Kennington Secondary Modern Boys' School. The lesson George learnt that day was that there were some things the English educational system could not teach him. For George, the system could only teach him what the system knew.

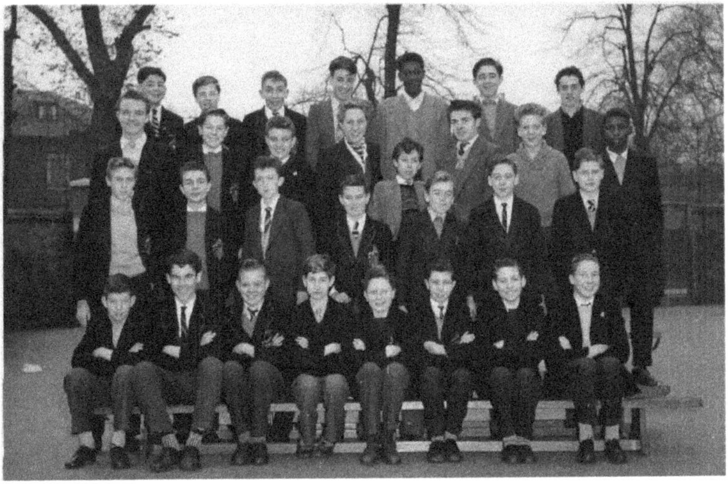

George and his classmates.
Kennington Secondary Modern Boys' School

COLD AND CHILBLAINS

George saw snow for the first time in 1957, the year he arrived in the UK. He woke up to find around four inches of brilliant white powdery snow covering the ground. George was elated as he trudged gingerly through the snow and ice on his way to school in his leather-soled shoes that had no grip. Sudden, unexpected slips and skids saw him trying desperately to keep his balance and stay upright at any cost!

When he got to the school gates, he saw a massive snowball fight being played out. It seemed that all the schoolboys were gleefully engaged in the snow showdown. George was so excited that he eagerly joined in the ongoing snowball brawl as soon as he entered the playground. Eventually, though, he had to stop, as his fingers felt like shards of ice.

Once in class, he sat at the back, where the radiators were. His hands were so cold from handling the snowballs that he placed them directly on the pipes to warm them up. As his hands began to thaw, his fingers became itchy and painfully red. He was probably experiencing chilblains for the first time. After that initial encounter with snow, George told his classmates that he would never touch snow again.

Two days later, when the snow changed into particles of slippery ice, another snowball fight began in the school playground, but this time, George refused to get involved. He remembered how numb his fingers had felt from his first snowball fight when the snow had been fresh. He smiled as he watched the boys duck and pelt snowballs at each other.

Suddenly, from out of nowhere, a snowball hit him full in the face, and then another quickly followed. Slowly, it dawned on him with emerging horror that he was the only one in the playground being targeted. Through the white mist of scattered snowballs falling around him, he could see that his friends were also throwing snowballs at him. He watched as the boys in the playground quietly gathered chunks of ice and solid crumbs, carefully shaping them into smooth round balls, almost as if time had slowed down. They felt like cricket balls when they fell perfectly on target on his face, ears, shoulders, back and chest—in fact, every area of his body!

George's eyes were drawn to the eager faces of his friends as they enthusiastically hurled snowballs at him, and he felt betrayed.

The cold spheres of ice rained down on him like a blizzard. Icy splinters slid down his neck through the tiny gap between his neck and his collar, trickling down into thin channels of freezing water soaking his chest.

George couldn't take the barrage of snowballs falling all around him any more. He looked over at the building site opposite, sprinted across the road, and quickly filled all the pockets of his duffle coat, bulging them to the brim with broken bricks. He boldly returned to the school playground with renewed vigour in his step.

Now, he eagerly took part in the fight, throwing rubble at the schoolboys with perfect aim, using his knowledge of bowling in cricket to slice and put a spin on the bricks and stones as he picked out his targets with expert precision. The boys scattered in all directions to the safety of the school building, and before long, it was just George standing alone in the playground. He could not understand why they had stopped hurling back snowballs in response to his broken bricks and stones, but that did not matter. He was just glad that he was not being pelted with snowballs anymore, and he felt triumphant!

Back in class, before the English teacher arrived, one of his friends said to him in a loud whisper, 'Ay, George, what was all that about? Why did you throw them bricks from the buildin' site? That wasn't a fair fight!'

George looked at him, leaned across Winston, and replied with a wry smile, 'Where me a come from, we don't throw ice. We fling bricks and stones!'

George expected to get in trouble for throwing bricks at his fellow pupils, but thankfully, that never happened, and he escaped punishment.

Another unpleasant experience George had during his first winter was dealing with chilblains. Along with the painful, itchy swellings on his fingers, he also had them on his toes. Chilblains are small, red bumps that primarily appear on the fingers and toes, but they can also affect areas like the earlobes, cheeks, heels, thighs, nose, shins and hips. Chilblains are caused when the skin is warmed up too quickly after being cold. That winter, it was extremely cold for George. Freezing, in fact. He was not sure how he got them, whether it was from going from warm rooms to cold areas of his school or coming in from the freezing cold into the warmer environment of his house. All he knew was that the itching was intense, and the only relief he had, though temporary, was when he scratched. The scratching reminded George of when he had been bitten by mosquitoes, and the area around the bite got inflamed and itchy. That was what chilblains felt like.

The pain and the scratching were relentless. George would scratch in front of the heater, in bed at night, first thing in the morning and sometimes, throughout the day. He only found relief when his wet flannel soothed and eased the pain, but that was only briefly. It was grim. His toes were constantly sore and itchy. George tolerated the pain, and eventually, the discomfort passed.

A paraffin heater was used to keep the house warm in the winter. Paraffin was poured into a small tank, and a match was used to light the circular wick that was protected by a grille. Most paraffin heaters only warmed up a small area of the room, so families would huddle around the fire, vying for the warmest spot. If you happened to leave your spot, it would quickly be taken. Should you return, you would be assigned to a colder part of the room. Many fights between siblings started over their space near the heater being taken.

Paraffin has a distinctive smell, and the odour permeated through the house. Later, more advanced paraffin heaters came on the market, which had a less distinctive smell and were more energy efficient, but some of the heaters were extremely unsafe. They could become a serious fire hazard, especially if they were knocked over and the paraffin was spilt.

Many cases of house fires occurred in the 1960s and early 1970s. The flames ignited by the paraffin instantly turned into a tsunami of flames, resulting in tragedies where, at worst, people died or had to live their lives with horrific memories and terrible scars from the burns they received. Sadly, some of the victims were children who'd played innocently near or knocked over the paraffin heaters.

Devastating fires also occurred when heaters were carried from room to room, whether by an adult or a child. If they tripped or the heater's handles became too hot to hold, the heater was hastily placed on the floor, causing the paraffin to spill and igniting the naked flame on the wick, resulting in the surrounding area catching alight. Despite the risks, this was the only way many people could afford to heat their homes.

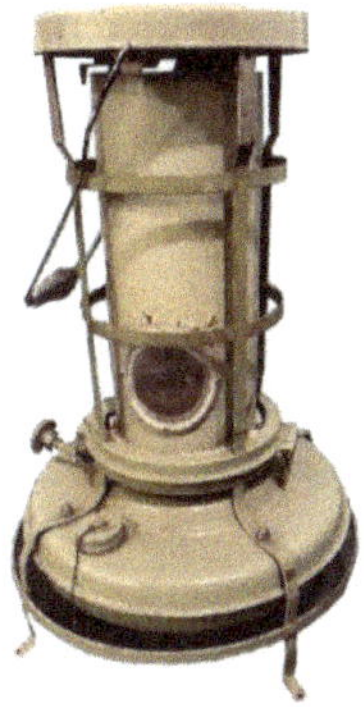

1970s Aladdin Paraffin heater

One evening, George filled the paraffin heater, but he overfilled the tank, causing the paraffin to spill onto the highly flammable floor covering. From his experience with kerosene in Jamaica, he knew that if it ever overflowed on the soil in the yard, he could use a lighted match to burn off the fuel, so this was what George instinctively did. He got the matches and lit the paraffin, thinking it would burn off, but instead, it set the linoleum alight. Horrified, George quickly grabbed a pillow and used it to smother the flames.

This was another valuable lesson in the difference between life in Jamaica and life in England that he had to get used to… and fast!

EMPLOYMENT

In the post-World War II era, jobs were plentiful. Hire Purchase was introduced, and families could afford to buy clothes and furniture 'on the never, never'. People would pay off their goods weekly or fortnightly, and they were able to take them from the shop. Many bought furniture, clothes, and larger items like televisions and radiograms. However, at Geneva Road, the furniture was provided by the landlord, and the only items George's parents bought on Hire Purchase were the television and the radiogram.

George was looking forward to leaving school to earn his own money. He admired how smartly dressed West Indians were, particularly his older male friends who had bespoke suits made by Jewish and Italian tailors in Brixton. George also looked admiringly at the 'Mods' and how they dressed as they rode around helmetless on their scooters, their girlfriends and friends riding pillion (a passenger seated at the back). However, he did not admire the style of the 'Rockers' who rode heavy motorbikes and wore tight jeans and leather jackets.

When George left school, he planned to save up money from his wages to buy himself a few smart suits and a scooter. Coming from a middle-class background, George was only interested in clerical or technical work, but there were certain jobs he would not lower himself to do, such as cleaning toilets.

In 1959, at the end of the 5th Year (Year 11), George left secondary school and signed on at the Youth Employment Bureau, also known as the Youth Labour Exchange (YEB), where you would be interviewed by a clerk and told of the available vacancies. After checking the applicant's qualifications and suitability, companies would be called to book interviews.

George's first job was as an apprentice projectionist at the Granada Cinema in Brixton, which has since been converted into a private housing development. He was excited about the chance to train as an engineer, a career he had always cherished. It was a profession his friends and neighbours had long believed he was destined for, ever since he was a young boy.

Most importantly, George was glad he would be independent, have his own money, and not have to rely on his parents.

As well as current movies, the cinema also showed Saturday morning pictures aimed at young children, such as cartoons, Westerns, Laurel and Hardy, Charlie Chaplin, and other films. During the interval, talent competitions took place on the stage in which the winners might be awarded small prizes. Many children accompanied their siblings and friends, often attending without a parent or guardian, some as young as five or six years of age. Their parents were either working, shopping, doing their chores, or having a lie-in while their children were at the cinema. In those days, it was relatively safe for children to travel independently. Children would attend Saturday morning pictures and return home by themselves.

George was excited to start his new job as an apprentice. Granada Cinema was an impressive building. It was originally named Empress Theatre and was built in 1898. In 1951, new management took it over, and it was renamed. The projection room, where the engineers worked, was at the uppermost part of the cinema. The height of the structure was equivalent to a six-storey building, but it had no lift, so taking the reels of film up to the projection room once a week was an arduous task.

The small team of three—consisting of a senior engineer, a junior engineer, and George, the apprentice—seemed friendly. The senior engineer was in his mid-forties, balding with greyish-brown hair, and he matter-of-factly explained George's duties, pointing out that, as a part of the terms of his apprenticeship, George would attend Brixton College twice a week. He would learn electrical engineering there, something George looked forward to qualifying in, and he smiled at the prospect of becoming a qualified engineer.

Martin, a slim ginger-haired man in his twenties, would train him. George looked intently at Martin, who nodded in unsmiling agreement at his boss's instructions. Despite assurances that Martin would train him on the projector, the training never happened, which did not surprise George. The only training George ever received was based on his observations and working out problems for himself.

In the beginning, he enjoyed the challenge of changing the reels and putting the films of the day on the projector. There were two projectors in the room, and the films automatically switched from one projector to the next. The lights were dimmed at the beginning of the screening and came back on when the film ended. An automatic switch opened and closed the curtains. These were the early days of computer-operated systems.

One afternoon, when George was left on his own as he often found himself, the automation malfunctioned, and there was complete chaos as the lights dimmed and brightened, the curtains opened and closed, and the projectors switched on and off. All of this happened in the middle of a screening! George struggled to fix the problem, and eventually, by sheer luck, he managed to get the automation under control. However, George soon lost his motivation from being left too often on his own to sort out problems that were sometimes hard to fix and occasionally, impossible.

He left the job after only two months for several reasons. One was that when the cleaners refused to climb the five floors to clean the projection room or the toilet, George, being the apprentice, was expected to do the tasks. Of course, George refused, which created tension. These issues, coupled with not being given time off to attend Brixton College to study electrical engineering, led him to resign.

Once again, George found himself at the YEB looking for work. A job that caught his eye was that of stock control clerk at British Railways Film Archives, Waterloo. The job involved collecting and filing documentary films held by British Rail. Excitedly, he took a bus to the interview, smartly dressed in an Italian navy blue suit that he bought from a tailor shop in Brixton; he wanted to give a good impression.

As part of the interview, George had to sit a basic English and Maths test, which he easily passed. He thought things were going well. The next stage was a face-to-face interview. He sat nervously in the waiting room, waiting to be called.

After what seemed like ages, he was directed to a white wooden door. On the door was a sign that said 'Manager'. He took a deep breath, knocked apprehensively on the door and entered when he heard, 'Come in.'

A man in his fifties sat behind a huge desk, pen in hand and a notepad in front of him. He looked up as George entered, but there was no welcoming smile. The manager looked George over, and, after what seemed like an eternity but was probably only a few seconds, he nodded towards a white wooden chair opposite him.

George sat down dutifully and, just as he tried to relax, the manager stated, 'You do realise this is not a job for coloured people.'

George was dumbfounded. The manager then put his head down quickly and started to write on the notepad, ignoring George's presence. That's when he realised the interview had come to an end.

He calmly and politely thanked the manager, got up and left the building in a daze. Had he really heard those words? What a waste of time and bus fare! It occurred to George that the manager had simply agreed to interview him out of obligation to the YEB.

Job rejections became so normal that it soon dawned on him that there was a 'colour bar' preventing people of colour from being employed in certain occupations. Unbeknown to the newcomers and George, it was legal for businesses to employ only people of pure European descent for certain jobs. People of colour were not always welcome to work in pubs, shops, as hairdressers, or even for some bus companies.

In 1963, there was a successful protest against the bus company Bristol Omnibus Company in Bristol, for such discrimination. This resulted in the infamous Bristol Boycott. It wasn't until 1965, however, that the Race Relations Act was passed, making it illegal to discriminate against people of colour by refusing them employment or housing.

Despite the difficulties he found in his search for work, George kept applying for jobs. He quickly became conscious of colour prejudice and realised that being a Black youth with ambition in London was not going to be easy for a teenager like him, as certain jobs would always be beyond his reach despite having qualifications and experience. However, the more interviews George attended, the more adept he became at anticipating whether he would receive a job offer or not based on the initial reactions of the interviewers. These knockbacks did not discourage George, as he was confident he would find work as jobs were plentiful. The motivation to earn his own money and be independent spurred his dogged determination not to give up. Undeterred, he carried on applying for jobs and going to interviews.

MUSIC

As a young man, George enjoyed working. Despite the setbacks, he was never out of a job, often walking out of one job and getting another quite quickly. After leaving his job at the cinema, he successfully applied for the post of stock control clerk in Margaret Street near Oxford Circus. He was paid £3 a week in cash, and with his newfound independence, he decided to buy a scooter. He enjoyed the social life and nightlife of Brixton but grew tired of waiting for buses to get around, and he felt that a scooter would be a better means of transport to get to work rather than the unreliable buses.

So, in 1959, his parents gave him some money for a deposit to buy a scooter. He knew exactly where to go. There was a car showroom on Walworth Road, that sold bubble cars, motorbikes and scooters.

He bought the scooter on a three-year Hire Purchase agreement and paid the monthly installments from his salary. He would go to the showroom and pay the instalments in the office, which was situated near East Street Market. The clerk recorded the amounts paid and updated him with the balance until the scooter was paid off.

Now that he was employed, George could afford to dress in the fashion of the time, and he became a Mod. When he went raving in clubs and parties, he wore clothing such as Italian-made suits, mohair suits, Wrangler jeans, T-shirts and brogues. In 1963, at the age of 18, George met Diane, and, a year later, they had a daughter, Caron. Unfortunately, the relationship ended when his daughter was very young, and Diane took their daughter back to Jamaica, periodically returning to London to visit George and his family.

After living for some time in rented accommodation, George's parents decided it was time to buy their own property. In those days, it was rare for banks and building societies to give mortgages to Black people, so the only means of acquiring mortgages was from the borough councils. Others bought their houses in cash from savings or via a pardner or a susu.

When George was 20 years old, his parents obtained a mortgage from Lambeth Council to buy a house. They purchased a two-storey home with a basement at 7 Crawshay Road, Brixton, in 1963. The houses were eventually acquired by Lambeth Council and demolished around 1971 or 1972 to make way for a new housing estate. That, too, has since been demolished, and another estate has been constructed with much more open space.

The neighbourhood had a large Black community, mainly made up of Jamaicans. It had three grocery stores selling Caribbean food. One of the shops was run by a family of Chinese Jamaicans. The street had the first Caribbean café, called Hilltop, and several illegal drinking clubs called 'shebeens', which the police raided from time to time, removing the illegal alcohol and beating up the customers and owners at will. Despite the risks, shebeen owners simply restocked in readiness for the next club event, and so the cycle was repeated: the police raided and the owners restocked, much to both parties' annoyance.

There were two sound systems in the neighbourhood. The DJs held dances and Blues parties (partygoers paid an entrance fee to a man at the door). The Blues parties took place in private homes, and the parties usually went on all night and into the early or late hours of the morning. It was not uncommon for Blues parties to go on till 6 or 8 a.m., and if it was a workday, partygoers would leave the parties, go home to freshen up, eat breakfast, and go straight to work. This was known as 'bleaching'. For George, Brixton was an amazing place to spend his late teens and early twenties.

He had his own apartment in their family's new house, which consisted of a bedroom area and sitting room, where he entertained friends and mainly played jazz and blues music. The house had a cellar, and the ever-resourceful George quickly transformed it into a rehearsal space. It was used by many musicians, including some who later became famous.

During the 1960s, George landed a job as a postman, which came with numerous benefits, including receiving driving lessons. He passed the driving test and was given a van. In addition to qualifying as a postman, George also had to learn all the counties and towns in the U.K., as well as the street names in the W1 area of London, which he also passed.

Being from Jamaica and loving the outdoors, George would sit outside on the front doorstep for any spare moment and marvel at his new surroundings and at the people as they went to and fro. It was on one of those days, a hot July afternoon, that, as George sat outside on the steep, greyish-white concrete steps, he glimpsed a figure he thought looked familiar, someone he recognised from Jamaica. He stared at the man as he went by, trying to recall exactly how he knew this person who looked similar to him in age. The young man was of a medium height and slim build and wore gold-rimmed glasses. He reminded George of someone who had gone to his primary school in Jamaica. The next time he saw the young man, George approached him and enquired, 'Hey man—did you go to Calabar Elementary School?'

He looked back at George with smiling brown eyes. The 20-year-old was surprised that George had even remembered him after all that time. He replied, 'Yeah, man,' with an unmistakable smile that lit up his handsome face. When the young man smiled, George instantly knew him: the man's name was Byron Lye-Fook.

He continued, 'I went there, and I do remember you. Our school was built by freed slaves from America in 1812.'

'Yes, that's right. I remember that story. We were always told that piece of history, too. We were told that our school was named after the town of Calabar, on the Calabar River in Iboland, Nigeria.' Before long, George and Byron were engaged in deep conversation, reminiscing about their time in Jamaica. That encounter developed into a friendship that lasted over the years and resulted in George becoming the godfather to one of Byron's sons,

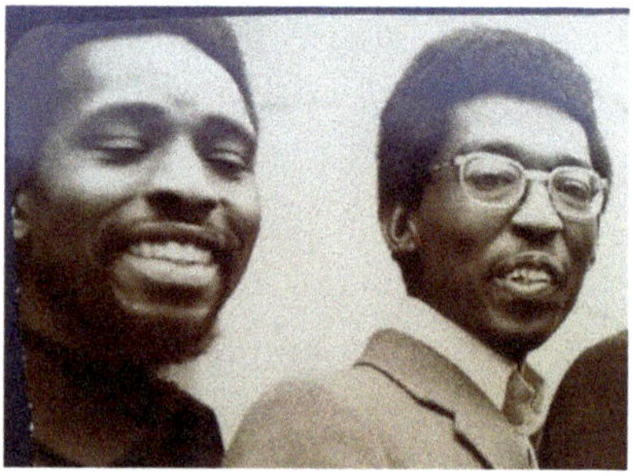

George and Byron

Kimon, the brother of the well-known singer-songwriter Omar. Byron's paternal grandfather, George Lye-Fook, had arrived in Jamaica from China (the year is unknown) and settled on the island, where he met a local woman called Florence. He stayed in Jamaica for several years before returning to China.

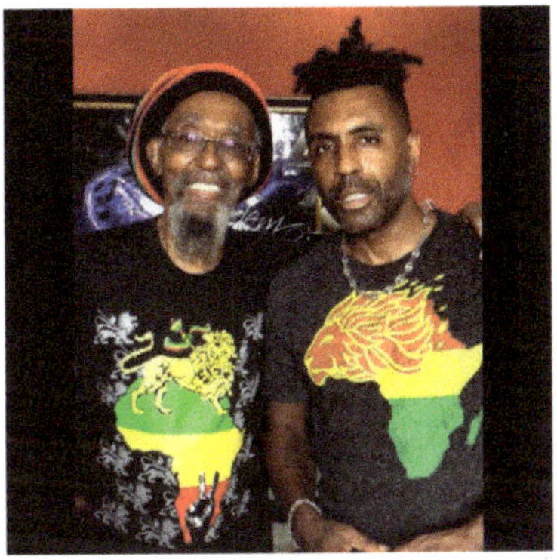
Byron and his son, Omar

At the time of the friends' reunion in Brixton, Byron played drums in a blues and rock 'n' roll band called The Dolphins, which, in addition to Byron, consisted of four white musicians who were in their late teens and early twenties. The band had no regular place to rehearse, so George offered the basement in his parents' house as a rehearsal space. The band was instrumental in helping George clean up the basement. Joe Limerick, the Dolphins' bass player, painted a huge picture of John Lee Hooker (an African-American blues singer) on a wall in the basement.

Byron's first band played rock and roll, but his second band played rhythm and blues, covering a range of songs by musicians such as Otis Redding, Booker T. and the MG's, Joe Tex, James Brown, Sam and Dave, and the like, as well as Motown songs, which were what most pop and soul bands sang at the time. When there were no bands playing in the basement, George held parties there for himself and his friends.

After a while, Byron gave up his job as a clerical assistant working in a tax office to become a full-time musician. Music became Byron's calling, and with his friend Root Jackson, he went on to start a record label in Harlesden called Congo Music, which was also a publishing company. The record label was later renamed Kongo Dance. Byron's band rehearsed regularly in George's parents' basement, and George would play alongside them, using his knees as a conga drum, beating them in time with the music.

Having constant music in the house inspired George. His musicality developed, and eventually, he acquired a conga drum and later a flute, the latter given to him by his girlfriend, Brenda Henderson, for his 23rd birthday. George soon became a new addition to the band. Ever resourceful, he started teaching himself to read music and play the congas and the flute, all of this despite holding down a full-time job as a postman. During this period of intense practise and learning two instruments, tension built up in George's body, and he needed a way of releasing it.

On a whim, George bought a bag of clay and found that squeezing and kneading hard lumps of clay helped. As time went on, he was left with large mounds of softened clay dotted around his room. Remembering his childhood years of making toys, a pastime he'd shared with his friends back in Jamaica, he started modelling figures using the clay. Little did he know that the skill of making figurines would one day become useful as he developed as a contemporary, creative artist.

Living in London, a young George and his Caribbean friends would go to the two most popular cinemas in the area: Pullmans' Cinema and the ABC (renamed The Fridge) in

Brixton. On Sundays, around 14 of them congregated outside of the ABC Cinema on Brixton Hill. They came from various parts of South London but were mainly from Brixton, Balham, Peckham, Catford and Lewisham. One Sunday in 1959, an incident happened inside the cinema that resulted in the young friends being barred.

As children in Jamaica, American gangster and cowboy movies were the genres George and his friends particularly enjoyed. The young men continued to behave as they had in the cinemas in the Caribbean. When the action films involved gunfights, George and his friends leapt out of their seats and loudly mimicked the sounds and behaviour of the action on the screen, screaming, '*Pow*! *Pow*!' as they reenacted the gunshots as well as adding to the film's dialogue with animated comments such as 'Lick 'em down,' 'Shoot 'em!' and more.

Naturally, this exuberant behaviour upset many of the white cinemagoers, and after one particular rowdy occasion, they were banned. Looking for somewhere else to go, they ended up in the West End. George's social life was transformed from that moment, as he discovered the nightlife of the West End: live jazz music at clubs like Ronnie Scott's, The Scene Club, where George first saw the Rolling Stones perform authentic-sounding blues music from the U.S.A., The Roaring Twenties Club on Carnaby Street, operated by a leading Sound System DJ called Count Suckle, blues and rock music at the Marquee Club on Wardour Street, and the Flamingo All Night Club, also on Wardour Street, where African-American GIs hung out.

In Brixton, George had little contact with Caribbean people who were not from Jamaica, but going to the clubs in the West End was the first time he met a wide variety of people from other parts of the West Indies: Grenadians, Trinidadians, Dominicans and St Lucians, travelling from places like Paddington, Ladbroke Grove and North London. He quickly learned to distinguish the individual accents from each island, but the most dominant accents he heard in the clubs were Jamaican and Trinidadian.

George, Byron and their friends went to see bands such as the Animals, Georgie Fame and the Blue Flames and Carl Douglas ('Kung Fu Fighting', 1974) live at The Flamingo Club. The music played was mainly rhythm and blues as well as soul. It was run by two brothers, who George thought were probably in their forties or fifties at the time, John Gunnel and his older brother, Rik. They also ran an artist-booking agency for artists from all over England.

The British youth culture in the 1950s and 1960s was heavily influenced by African-American and Jamaican music. Teenagers loved the new dances and fashions from across the Atlantic. Artists such as the Beatles and the Rolling Stones, amongst many other rock musicians, were also heavily influenced by the music.

The music played by the sound systems brought the culture from Jamaica and American cities like Chicago, Detroit (Motown) and New Orleans to Britain. During that time, several British bands sprang up, such as The Rudies and The Foundations. The Equals, featuring Eddie Grant's song 'Baby, Come Back', with his mixture of soul and rock 'n' roll, reached number one in the British charts in 1968. This explosion of Black British music influenced by Black Americans and Jamaicans happened at the same time as the start of the musical careers of George, Byron and Sam, George's brother.

Chris Blackwell, a white Jamaican, founded Island Records in London and was behind the growth of reggae and British rock music. He managed many famous groups of the day, such as The Spencer Davis Group (featuring Steve Winwood), Bob Marley, Jimmy Cliff, and Millie Small, singer of the hit song 'My Boy Lollipop'.

When the clubs finished at 6 a.m., George got on his scooter and rode home with one of his friends, usually Byron, riding pillion. They didn't wear helmets until it became law in 1973. Once he got home, he went straight to work after a wash and a bite to eat.

George met a wide variety of Caribbean people when he was in the clubs and at his job at the Post Office. He quickly made friends with some Jamaicans and Trinidadians who were also part-time musicians. When they heard that George had a basement where bands rehearsed, they wasted no time in asking him if they could use the space.

As time passed, George began to think that his Post Office friends, who practised regularly in his parents' basement, were talented enough to perform professionally. Inspired by this, he came up with the idea of forming a band, and they decided to call themselves *Dem Guys*. George managed the group, arranging club bookings and promotions, and bought a van to drive them to gigs. The band fluctuated between seven and eight members. Inevitably, there were conflicts when the Trinidadians wanted to play calypso, and the Jamaicans wanted to play reggae. However, their London audiences were mostly Mods who wanted to hear reggae and soul music, and when they played in cities like Birmingham, the young—mostly white—audience only wanted to hear reggae. Eventually, constant disagreements amongst the band members about which music genre should be played caused the band to split up.

Sam was a drummer in another band, and when the band needed a conga player, he suggested George, who was available because he was no longer managing Dem Guys. Coincidentally, George was made redundant from the Post Office at the same time, so he could devote all his time to the band. Soon after he joined his brother's band, they changed their name to Cymande, though by the time they had launched their first album, George had left.

The band went on tour around the East Coast of America, and on their return, they asked George to come back as tour manager for their next U.S. tour. The tour was a success, and on the back of that, the world-famous reggae artist Jimmy Cliff employed George to become a sound engineer for his first tour of Nigeria in 1974. This tour resulted in a series of experiences that would change the direction of George's life.

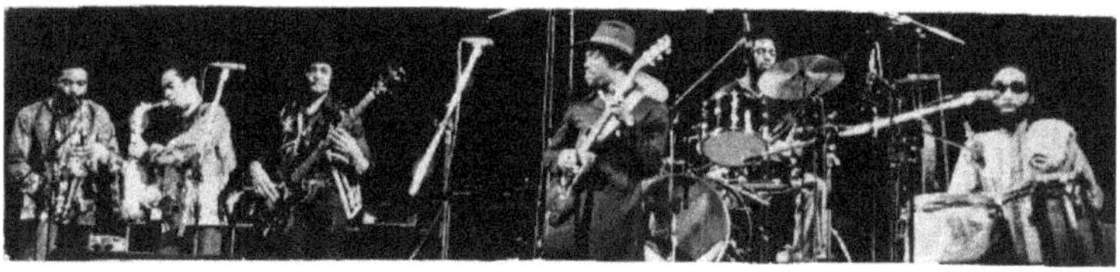

Cymande

DESTINY AND FATE

In the mid-1970s, Lagos was the capital of Nigeria, but the capital was later moved to Abuja in the centre of the country. At the time, Lagos had a rapidly growing population of several million people. Upon seeing so many Black people in such large numbers, George was enthralled with the familiarity of their faces and body language. He felt as though he was in the countryside of Jamaica.

George looked forward to starting his two-week job as a sound engineer for Jimmy Cliff's band, which involved mixing the instruments and vocals to balance the sound. Lagos, where the tour started, is in the southwest. The tour continued to Port Harcourt in the east, then north to Kano. The band's first gig was at the stadium in Lagos, where the special guest was Fela Ransome-Kuti (or simply Fela or Fela Kuti), the godfather and creator of Afrobeat.

The band travelled to the rest of the gigs in a convoy that consisted mainly five or six estate cars. At the time, there were few paved highways outside Lagos, and there were mainly dirt roads. To get to the gigs, the band travelled hundreds of miles along the dusty and bumpy roads through endless palm forests.

They saw flaring oil wells billowing smoke as well as lone teenage boys with long sticks controlling herds of cattle in the Islamic north and watched admiringly at the roaming wild camels.

The highlight of the tour, not only for George but also for the band, was going to the Palace of the Oba of Benin, the temporal ruler of the Edo people. The band remained in the palace's grounds while the lead singer had an audience with the Oba. The visit was important for George because the Kingdom of Benin was the original home of the famous Benin Bronzes. He was awestruck! Having seen the high-quality craftsmanship of the Benin Bronzes at the Horniman Museum in London, he felt privileged to be in the palace grounds.

A substantial amount of the Oba's bronze collection had been looted by the British when they invaded Benin City. This became known as the 'Benin Punitive Expedition', which began on 9 February 1897.

The King of Benin was captured and stripped of his titles. His treasures were looted and sold to museums and collectors around the world, who marvelled at the rich cultural legacy the Africans had created. The British Museum and the Horniman Museum in London house some of these treasures.

At the end of the Jimmy Cliff tour, the band members left Kano and returned to London. However, it was George's job to stay behind and return the musical equipment to the U.K. Once the equipment arrived and was processed, George reflected on his time in Africa and the positive experience of being in Nigeria. He expected to see the poverty caused by the civil war between Biafra and the Nigerian government represented in the media, such as the undernourished children and poor-quality

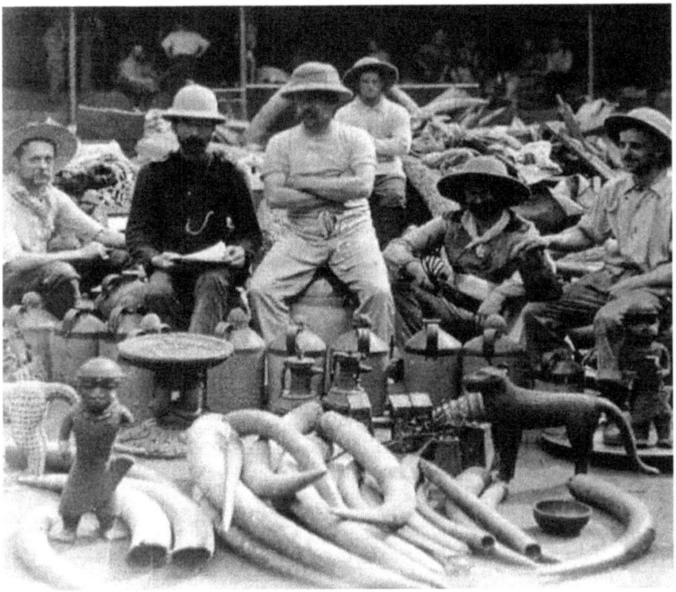

© Alamy Stock Photo

British colonial soldiers with the loot from the Kingdom of Benin

housing shown regularly on television, but where he visited, this was not the case. In fact, he saw the opposite. The people he saw were neither poor nor undernourished.

He was looking forward to going back to London to share his experiences, as being on his own without the band made him feel lonely. He also missed his mother. He imagined that she would have loved to have seen Africa, the land of her ancestors and from where her first name originated. He didn't worry too much as he would see her soon enough.

However, a few days before his flight was due, George rang the airline to confirm his return flight to London only to discover, to his dismay, that his airline ticket had been cancelled. He had no money and no means of buying another plane ticket, as he had spent what he had on souvenirs. The band had left, so there was no one George could turn to for help. He was stranded!

Being sociable was an asset George had in abundance, and fortunately, he had made friends with one of the Nigerian members of the touring party, called Shola. Not wanting George to be destitute and homeless, she found accommodation for him at her sister's home, where he stayed for a short while.

Again, fortune and fate were on his side, and, by chance, George became friendly with a Caribbean woman, Marian, whom he met during a night out at Fela Kuti's nightclub, The Shrine. Marian and her sister invited George to stay in their home with their two children, and he quickly became close to Marian's partner, who was a university professor. The professor came from a wealthy family. He was a lecturer at the University of Ibadan in Nigeria, and his previous jobs included lecturing at universities in Addis Ababa, Ethiopia, Cambridge University in England, and the University of Chicago in the U.S.A. The two men had regular debates on world politics, African cultures, and how the people of the Caribbean still practised African traditions.

One evening, after one of their regular chats, the professor inquired, 'George, do you want to remain in Nigeria or go back to England?' George thought for a moment about his family, whom he had not contacted because he was too embarrassed about the predicament he was in. He hated being in that position, not knowing how he would ever afford to return to England.

He grew quiet, and in a voice that was almost a whisper, he struggled to hold back the lump in his throat as he replied, “Yes, I do want to go back to England, but...” George’s words faded. He thought of his mother, who would be frantic with worry, having received no news from her older son. When he looked up, he found the professor staring at him, his gaze fixed and intense.

The professor caught George’s eyes and simply nodded, likely having seen the pain and anxiety on George’s face. He had grown fond of his Jamaican friend, and although he enjoyed his company and would miss him if he left, he knew it was time for George to return to England.

Several days after George’s conversation with the professor, an airline ticket appeared on the coffee table. The professor pushed the ticket towards George.

‘What’s this?’ George enquired as he picked up the ticket.

‘It’s for you,’ the professor responded. ‘It’s your ticket back to London.’

George was overcome with gratitude and disbelief. He thanked the professor profusely, grateful for his generosity, and stared at the airline ticket with a mixture of disbelief and appreciation. After spending three months in Nigeria and living with the professor’s family for five weeks, George was finally going back to England. He could barely contain his excitement.

As George packed his belongings, he stopped to admire the souvenirs he had bought. He was taking some treasured items with him back to England. As he travelled through parts of Nigeria, he was amazed by the traditional arts and crafts on sale, such as busts, clay pots, animal sculptures, and carvings. Also on sale were some atypical arts and crafts, made specifically for tourists, like spears, which are not used in Nigeria but were made for tourists, who stereotypically thought that was what Africans used. The items were sold by informal traders along the roadside, in markets, on beaches and anywhere tourists could be found. George marvelled at the artistry of the talented people who had created these items, who had never been to art school or attended higher education. He would sometimes stop to buy and talk to the traders, share experiences and hear how the artefacts were made, as well as the cultural traditions and history behind their creations.

George felt a connection to the traders who'd created the artworks. Some had been self-taught, and they shared their knowledge with George about how they had developed their skills without any formal training. This resonated with George, as he, too, had taught himself to play the flute and conga. He drew parallels between Jamaican and Nigerian traditions, as well as the way children and those in their early teens made toys by observing and imitating adults at work, much like him and his friends.

A new wave of creativity came alive in George. He knew that when he got back to England, he would make changes to his life. The inspiration he got from his travels made him think hard about the direction his life should take.

NEW DIRECTIONS

After his first trip to West Africa, when George returned to England in 1975, he brought Nigeria's energy and spirit with him. Seeing the amazing sculptures at the Oba's palace was the main motivation to look life—one that would be centred on art rather than music.

The energy and spirit of Nigeria, especially in Lagos, was something George had never experienced before or since. He began used this energy to develop his artistic passions.

Amongst the souvenirs George brought back from his trip was a pair of sandals made from car tyres. He had bought these from informal traders on Lagos' waterfront. The sandals were like the ones worn by early Rastas in Jamaica in the 1930s and 1940s, which they called '*sampatas*' or '*power*'.

Byron liked the sandals George wore. He looked admiringly at them and asked, 'You can make a pair for me nah, man?'

George was not sure, but he told Byron he would think about it. He'd grown up in the 1940s and 1950s, a period when people made many of the toys we take for granted today such as bicycles, dolls, etc., so when George got home, he scrutinised each sandal closely. He thought he could easily make them. Despite having never made a pair of sandals before, he set about making some for his friend.

The following day, George went to the local secondhand tyre shop. Luck was once again on his side, as he did not need to buy any—he was directed to a pile of discarded tyres. His first foray into making sandals was a bit of a failure as the tyres he initially acquired had steel wire inside, which made cutting them with a Stanley knife impossible. However, his perseverance paid off, and George realised there were tyres with nylon threads. These, he found, were easier to cut and shape. To make the sole, he cut the rubber with either a sharp knife or a Stanley knife, depending on what was at hand. He used the inner tube from the tyre to make the strap but later used leather instead of inner tubes. Before long, he had made a pair of sandals. Thus began George's career as a craftsperson.

Through word of mouth, the sandals he made became very popular, and they eventually came to the attention of Sir Lloyd Coxsone, who was one of the top London sound system operators of the time. He asked George to make some sandals for him and his posse for the upcoming Notting Hill Carnival. George saw an opportunity—if the sound system crew wore the sandals, then their massive number of followers might be interested in buying them, as well. So, at the 1975 Notting Hill two-day carnival, George hired a stall to sell sandals and T-shirts with printed images of the sandals on them.

The carnival saw a huge crowd of people who danced and frolicked, following the steel bands playing the calypso music that emanated from the floats. Groups in carnival costumes, as well as revellers, danced to the stationary music coming from the numerous sound systems, playing a range of R 'n' B, reggae, soul and disco music. When the revellers passed by

George's stall, many stopped to buy or look at his sandals, and by the end of day one, half of his stock was sold. At the end of day two, he had an even smaller number of unsold sandals. He hoped his Jewish friend, Ari, who owned a shop on Portobello Road, would be interested in selling his unsold goods.

The next morning, George took a bus to Portobello Road, and after a brief chat, he casually asked Ari if he would sell the sandals. Ari was interested and said that he could sell them in his shop, especially to the hippy community living in the Notting Hill area at the time.

'George, you could make a lot of money from these sandals,' Ari said wisely and prophetically. 'Could you create a poster that would describe the sandals?'

Though he was surprised by the request, George tried to act confidently. 'Sure, Ari. No problem!' With a sense of determination, George reassured Ari that he would, formulating plans in his mind on how to fulfil his friend's request.

As George made his way home, he mentally went through the stages of how he would create the poster, pondering how he could use his cultural background to illustrate the historical significance of the sandals worn by the early Rastas.

George created a silkscreen poster of a Rasta man's head framed inside a tyre (which was later stolen from his friend's shop). He enjoyed making the poster so much that it opened a whole new world for him. He went on to develop silkscreen prints in a fresh and emerging market. His posters were four-colour, silkscreen prints, whereas, at the time, silkscreens were usually only two colours. This enabled him to use the Rasta colours of red, gold, black and green in his designs. George began to create T-shirts and cultural posters that represented

African images, Rasta belts from wool and Rasta jewellery from coconut shells and leather.

At the same time George was making these items, he also taught himself how to create sculptures. The success of the sandals at the 1975 Notting Hill Carnival gave George the confidence that he should sell his goods again at the following year's carnival, but the next time, he would sell a wider variety of his handmade goods.

The Black Power movement arrived in America in the 70s. It was a movement that positively promoted people of colour in order to change the negative images of Black people portrayed in books and the media. African-styled fashion became popular amongst Rastas and the culturally conscious. People flocked to buy products that identified with African culture. Coincidently, the jewellery, T-shirts, belts and crafts George was making were amongst the popular goods people wanted to buy.

The summer of 1976 was the hottest on record. It was also the year of street battles between young people and the police at the Notting Hill Carnival. Fortunately, George had sold most of his goods at the carnival before the violence erupted. He was able to collect the few items that remained and left quickly to avoid the mayhem.

A variety of cultural shops sold arts and crafts in the 1970s, so George used this opportunity to sell his works on a sale-or-return basis. Bogle L'Ouverture in Ealing and Sabaa Book Shop in Brixton were two of the bookshops where he sold his jewellery, posters, sandals and T-shirts, which helped pay his bills.

THE MAKING OF A MASTERPIECE

George's sales from the carnival generated a small surplus, which meant he could buy a lot more equipment and materials to begin making sculptures. His experience of being in Nigeria inspired him to connect with his African heritage, and he wanted to express this through sculpting.

George began thinking about how he was going to start, reflecting on the fact that he had always had an innate interest in art. This had deepened following a school trip to the Horniman Museum and during his trip to Nigeria, where he saw amazing African 3D models being exhibited. His interest in classical European art developed after a visit to the National Gallery in Trafalgar Square. He was also attracted to the art of ancient Egypt, Greece and Rome. His recent journey to Africa and his introduction to the ancient bronze culture of Ife and Benin combined to lay the foundation for his future creativity.

Even though George had no experience creating sculptures and had only attended three art lessons in secondary school, it seemed easy enough to do, so he gave it a go. His goal was to make works of art in 3D. High-quality African art was being made by exceptionally skilled artists who'd spent many years being trained as apprentices under a master. If he failed, so what? He would keep trying until he made a piece that was just as good as the sculptures he admired.

In 1976, when George was 33 years old, he began teaching himself how to create sculptures. He did not go to any workshops or academic institutions to be taught. Instead, he spent all of his free time experimenting with a variety of materials such as wax, wood, clay and plaster to hone and perfect his skills.

His determination eventually paid off, and he began producing pieces in wood. The first carved piece was an African mask, spear and shield on balsa wood. It took many years of experimentation and trial and error to create artwork George was satisfied with. Ultimately, he was working towards creating a piece he could describe as his masterpiece, which was a bust in the style of the Ife Bronze culture. He felt that moment of achievement would require him to take on a new name that would show his transition from learner to master, so George adopted the African name of Fowokan. The Yoruba word *fowokan* means 'one who creates with the hand'.

Now, Fowokan George Kelly creates his 3D sculptures by first selecting individuals based on their distinctive facial features, either through his imagination or from images that appear in his dreams. He uses meditation to imagine the sculpture in its 3D form and creates the piece, first in clay, then he makes a mould and casts the piece in a permanent material, such as epoxy resin or metal.

When he started creating 3D pieces, some people were not accustomed to seeing African people positively represented in artwork. Some were uncomfortable and thus avoided looking at them. One gallery described his work as being 'too tribal' and rejected them.

Fowokan George Kelly has been practising art for over 50 years and feels that it is now time to pass the baton on to the next generation of artists and young people who have a dream but who have not had the opportunity, help or the motivation to realise their talent.

As a way of giving back, Fowokan runs workshops in primary and secondary schools as well as with university students. With older students, he gives talks explaining the techniques and inspiration behind his work, as well as its historical origins. Fowokan believes that Black people have a duty to tell their stories, as no one else can. He feels they must endeavour to take on the responsibility of telling that story, which is what he continues to do through his work and the talks he gives. Fowokan possesses a unique gift, and his journey as a self-taught artist is a story that deserves to be celebrated. He is proud to have had the opportunity to showcase his sculptures in prestigious galleries in the U.K., the U.S.A. and Cuba.

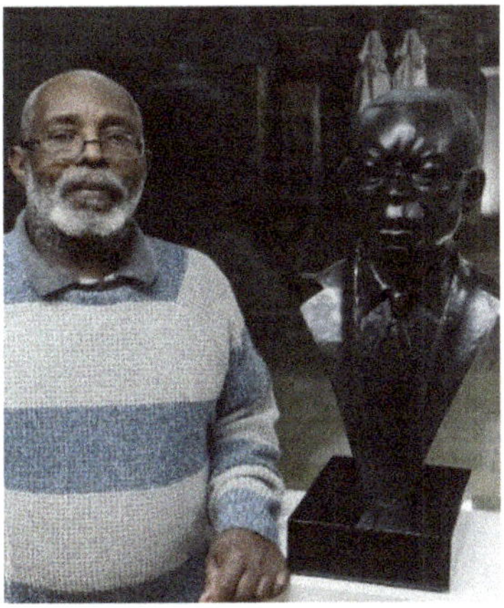

The model of Len Garrison exhibited at The Black Cultural Archives in Brixton

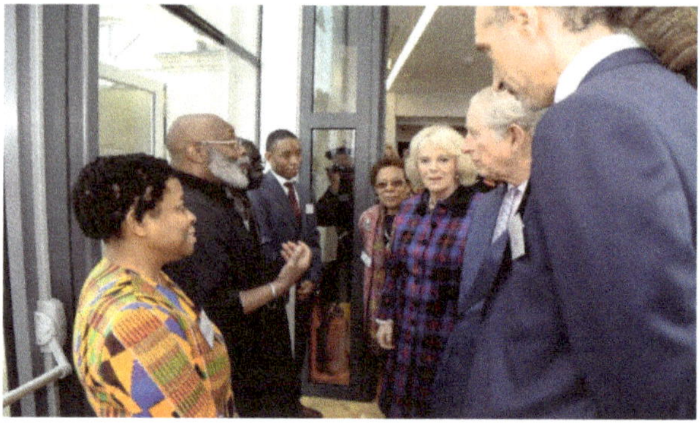

© Charlie Phillips 20.02. 2017

Fowokan George Kelly, Marie Garrison, Tunde Garrison, Prince Charles and Camilla at The Black Cultural Archives, Brixton

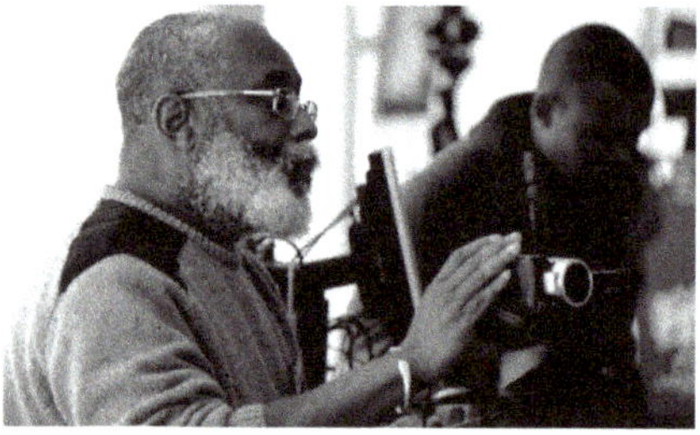

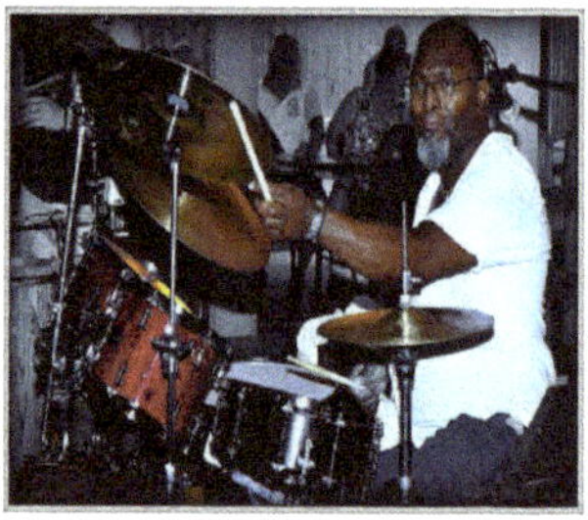

Sam Kelly

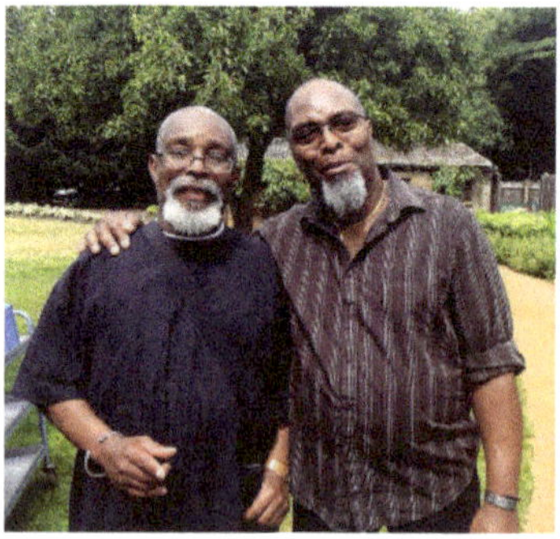

Fowokan George Kelly and Sam Kelly

LONA, SHE WHO CAME TO PREPARE THE WAY

In 2017, Fowokan had the honour of meeting Prince Charles (now King Charles III) during a visit to the Black Cultural Archives (BCA) in Brixton. During the encounter, Prince Charles listened as Fowokan explained the creative process behind his bust of Len Garrison, the late founder of the BCA and a close friend. Today, Len's bust proudly stands on display at the BCA.

Later that same year, Fowokan also had the privilege of meeting the Ooni of Ife, the spiritual leader of the Yoruba people, on another visit to the Black Cultural Archives. Reflecting on these moments, Fowokan felt deeply moved, knowing he had encountered two of the most significant leaders connected to his heritage (The Oba of Benin and The Ooni of Ife)—an experience he had never imagined witnessing in his lifetime.

Artistic and Creative Pursuits

Fowokan's talents extend far beyond sculpture. He has written poetry since the age of 13, a passion that remains integral to his life. Photography also captivated him at a young age—his first camera, a Kodak Brownie, was a cherished birthday gift that sparked a lifelong fascination. Over the years, he has documented his travels, community events, and his own creative processes, sharing some of these videos online to great acclaim.

His art and creativity have reached wide audiences, with his works featured on BBC's *Artsnight* (2014) and Channel 4's *The Empire Pays Back* (2005). His website, www.fowokan.com, has amassed over 9 million hits, a testament to the global appreciation of his work.

Family and Connections

Fowokan's daughter Caron was the first in the family to attend university, earning a degree in English Literature from the University of the West Indies and a Law degree from the University of East London. Tragically, she suffered a severe stroke in 2008 at the age of 45, leaving her unable to work. However, her determination and accomplishments have left a lasting legacy. Her daughter, Che, now in her twenties, continues this legacy, having earned a degree in Criminology.

Fowokan has shared his journey with his partner, Margaret Andrews, whom he met in 1985. Margaret is an accomplished author, a former secondary school teacher, and a former director at Hackney Community College. Together, they have travelled extensively, visiting countries across Africa, the Caribbean, Europe, Asia, and the Americas. Of all their travels, Fowokan holds a special fondness for Nigeria, which reminded him of Jamaica in the 1940s, the time of his boyhood.

Legacy of Family

Neither of Fowokan's parents lived to see the full scope of their children's successes. His father passed away in 1965 at the age of 61, while his mother, Lona, died in 1991. Despite this, their influence and nurturing spirit have left an indelible mark. Lona, whose Yoruba name means ‘ one who comes to prepare the way,’ lived up to her name, paving the path for her sons and future generations.

Fowokan’s aunt, lovingly known as Auntie Lyn, played a significant role in encouraging the family’s ambitions. She passed away in Jamaica in 1998 but was filled with pride for Fowokan and his brother Sam, frequently updated on their achievements.

The Kelly Legacy

Sam Kelly, a renowned blues drummer, is celebrated internationally for his contributions to music. He continues the family tradition of success, sharing it with his son Ronnie (DJ Skol), a globally recognised entertainer.

Both parents would undoubtedly have been immensely proud of their sons’ achievements, especially their father, who attended school only until the age of eight. Their decision to bring their sons to England was driven by the hope of providing them with greater opportunities—a hope that has been fully realised.

A Legacy of Resilience and Triumph

The journey of Fowokan and his family stands as a testament to resilience, creativity, and determination. From the West Indies to England, and from humble beginnings to international recognition, their story is a vivid example of success built on the foundation of love, sacrifice, and shared ambition. You could say it truly was a job well done.

MARGARET'S STORY

It was in the summer of 1985 that Margaret met George. At the time, she was part of a women's group called MELJJINA. The name is an acronym formed by the initials of the women in the group: Margaret, Ebun, Liz, and Jenny (Anita). 'Ina' was taken from the Swahili '*jina*', meaning 'collective'. MELJJINA sold African-themed crafts, books, toys, household items and clothing. The members of the group were all working mothers with young children. Margaret was a single parent of an 18-month-old daughter, Shani. Along with other members of the group, they set up a business to provide positive Black images for children, both in their homes and in schools.

The organisation sold their goods to friends and family as well as at craft markets, such as the Albany in Deptford, the Portobello Docks and the Lyric Theatre, Hammersmith. All members of MELJJINA were active in purchasing stock; however, as a full-time teacher, Margaret was only available to do her share of buying and selling stock on weekends, evenings and school holidays.

Through a contact, Margaret heard about a sculptor called Fowokan George Kelly, who made crafts and jewellery, items that were perfect for MELJJINA to purchase for their craft markets. So, on a hot July afternoon in 1985, together with her friend, Ebun, they both made their way to Fowokan's ground floor flat in Tulse Hill to buy his sculptures to sell at their craft stall at an upcoming market.

He greeted them at the door, and they followed the shoeless Fowokan to his living space. The musty smell of Fowokan's bachelor flat—a combination of washing and drying over several days, cooked food and the pleasant metallic aroma of a mixture of clay, resin and paints—engulfed Margaret and Ebun's nostrils as they entered.

Fowokan's open-plan flat was deliberately sparsely furnished to accommodate his art. At one end was a fitted kitchen, and at the other end was a balcony that led into the communal garden area. At the end of the garden was a gate leading to Brockwell Park, Brixton.

There was a large desk with a filing cabinet for storage, and two chairs were neatly arranged around a table at the opposite end of the room, which was the living room, situated next to the bedroom.

A corner of the desk was filled with containers, mainly empty, washed tomato cans filled with paintbrushes, carving tools, pencils and pens. There were silkscreen prints, wood carvings on the walls and other 3D sculptures and carvings scattered around the flat.

Margaret and Ebun marvelled at the exquisite sculptures on display throughout the flat. They were even more impressed when Fowokan told them he had made the pieces himself. Fowokan explained that he had made models as a young boy in Jamaica, and the inspiration to create sculptures came when he visited Nigeria in 1974.

They saw large sculptures of various sizes, from 30 cm to a metre high, but they were not for sale as they were a part of Fowokan's personal collection. They also saw items they felt would be popular amongst their target market, such as pewter brooches, necklaces, woven bamboo Rasta jewellery, and belts in red, black, green and yellow.

Margaret and Ebun felt that the cost of Fowokan's art was much higher than the prices their MELJJINA customers were likely to pay. However, his amazing works of art were too good to leave. Although costly, they hoped potential buyers would be attracted by the quality of his work and make a purchase or several purchases. Fowokan offered them a selection of his smaller sculptures on a sale or return basis. In addition to the sculptures, he gave them Rasta-coloured and copper-plated jewellery, such as earrings and necklaces, free of charge. As Fowokan was no longer making and selling jewellery, he was happy to give them away to create space for other artworks he had made or was going to make.

Margaret was taken by his generosity. She was intrigued by him and his independence, historical and cultural knowledge, and his steely focus on his passion, art. He offered his visitors mint tea (which Margaret later realised was the only refreshment he had).

As they sipped the herbal tea, Fowokan told them about the work he had produced and the difficulty of selling works to Black people who looked 'African'. He found that some Black people would rather buy European images than those that reflected themselves. Margaret and Ebun said that they, too, had shared the same experience, but unlike him, they received a monthly salary, Margaret from teaching and Ebun from her job as a social worker, whereas Fowokan solely relied on selling his arts and crafts to survive.

Of all the artists and suppliers whose stock MELJJINA bought, Fowokan was the only person who allowed them to take his artworks on a sale or return basis. He became a good contact for stock, and Margaret gradually became the main person with whom he communicated. However, after almost a year, they were unable to sell any of Fowokan's sculptures. Customers had shown interest and made positive comments, but they were either not prepared or could not afford to buy them. Out of respect for his art and his generosity, Margaret purchased one of his pieces and returned the unsold items to him, as it was clear that although he had exquisite and unique works of art, MELJJINA would not be able to sell any of his sculptures.

When Margaret returned the items, Fowokan realised that he might not have the opportunity to see her again. He liked her—she was intelligent, interesting and beautiful—and he did not want to lose contact with her, so he asked her out on a date. It so happened that the date he chose was Valentine's Day, so on 14 February 1986, Fowokan went with Margaret to dinner. It was the meeting that marked the start of a long and interesting relationship.

After MELJJINA stopped trading, Margaret helped promote Fowokan's artwork. She believed in his work and felt as if many people would purchase it; his work just needed to be seen. So, Margaret spread the word about his jewellery and sculptures among her family, friends and the organisations with which she volunteered. This increased Fowokan's network of customers and brought him several new clients who began buying his jewellery. A few customers even commissioned him to create jewellery in gold and silver. He also sold quite a few of his small sculptures, and a few clients bought his larger sculptures, for which they paid in instalments. Although Fowokan did not make large sums of money from his sales, it was just enough to get by.

In the mid-90s, Margaret and Fowokan began working together preparing printed information for his exhibitions; Fowokan wrote the words, and Margaret edited. That collaboration continues to this day. After almost four decades of travelling across the U.K., Europe and Africa, Fowokan and Margaret are still together.

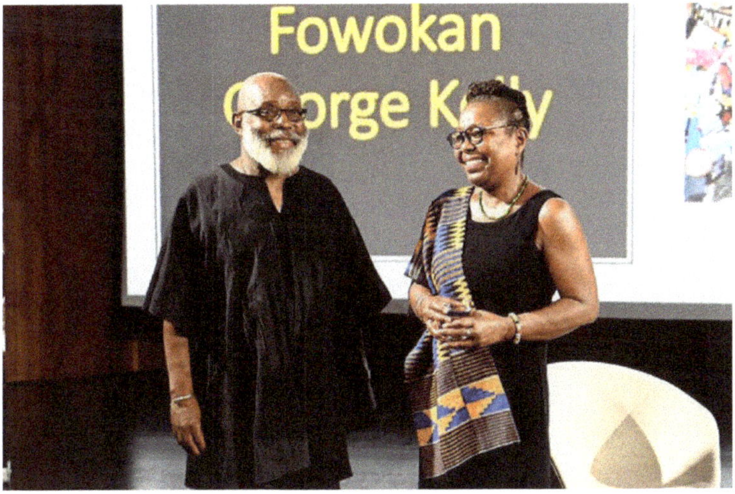

Fowokan George Kelly and Margaret Andrews

THE FOWOKAN'S WORKS AND IMAGES

Fowokan has birthed many works throughout his career, some of which are captured over the next few pages.

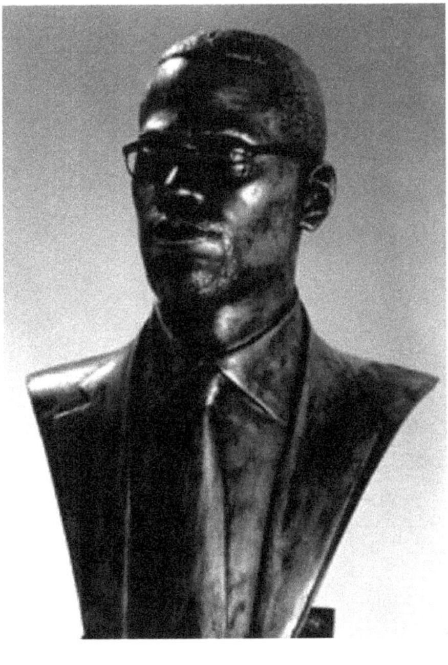

Malcolm X

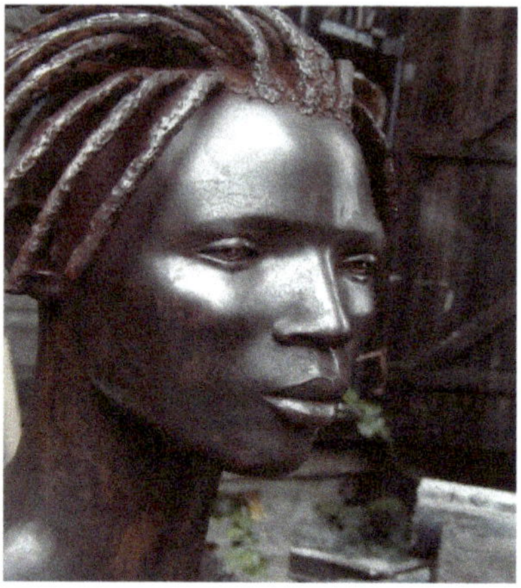

Carriacou Woman

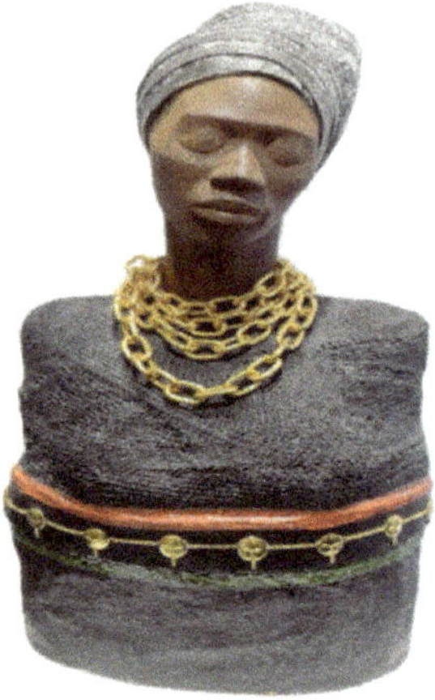

Mitochondrial Eve

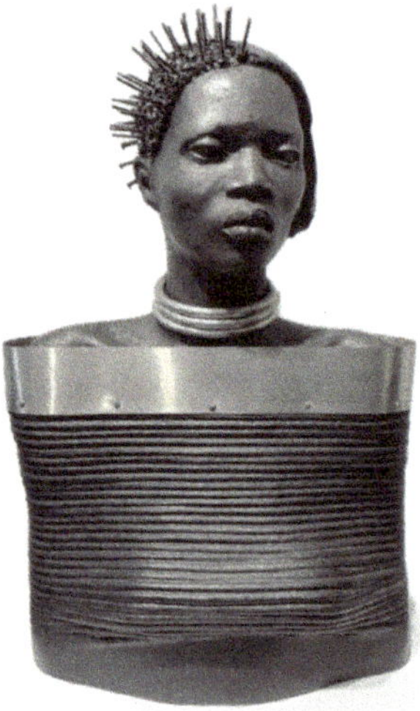

Lost Queen of Pernambuco

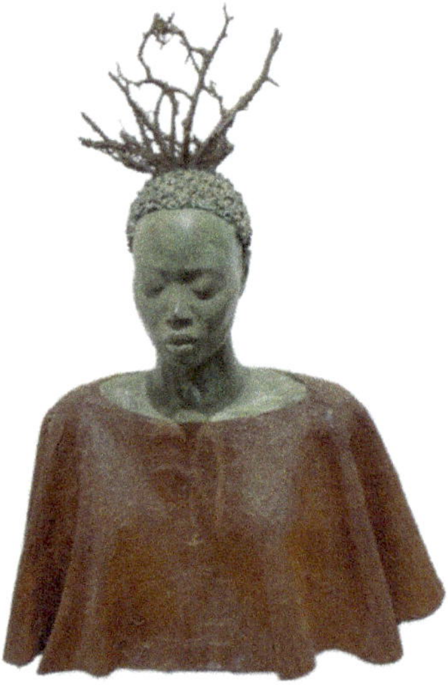

Olokun Mother
of the Deep Ocean

A small selection of the jewellery Fowokan has made:

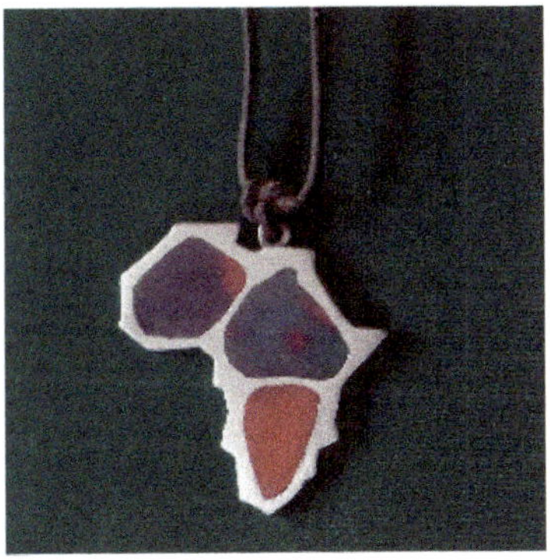

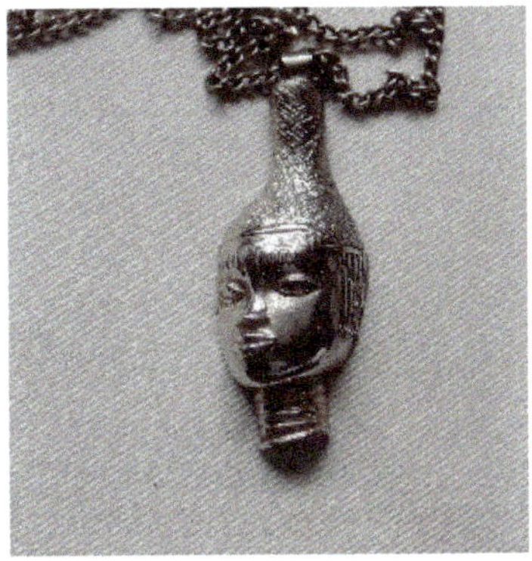

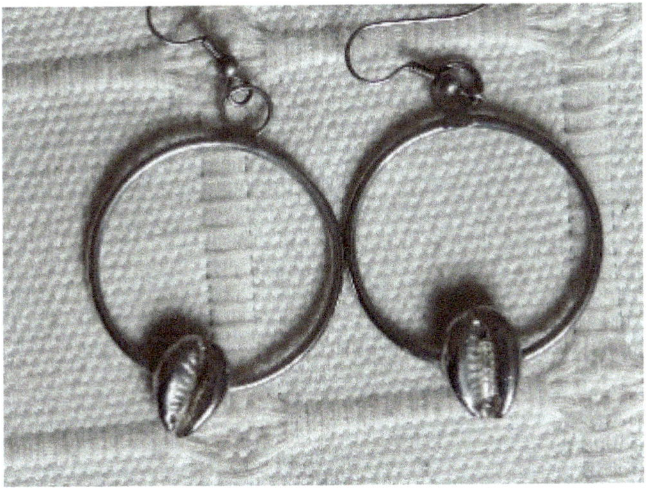

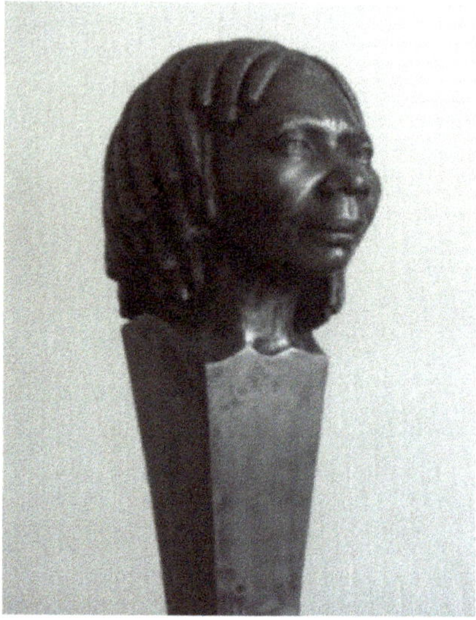

Jessica Huntley
Race Equality Campaigner and Founder of Bogle-L'Ouverture Publications (1969)

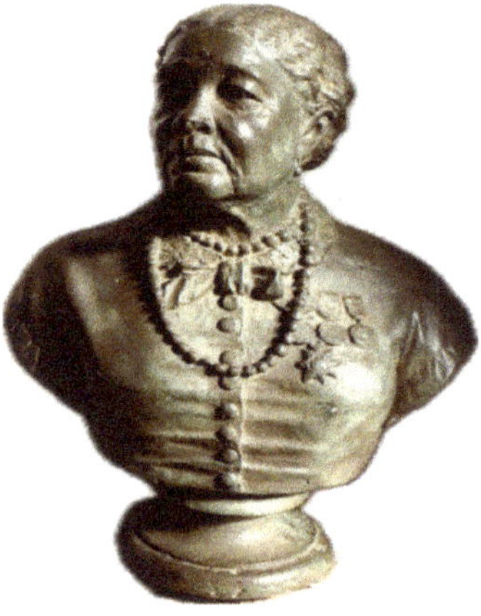

Mary Seacole

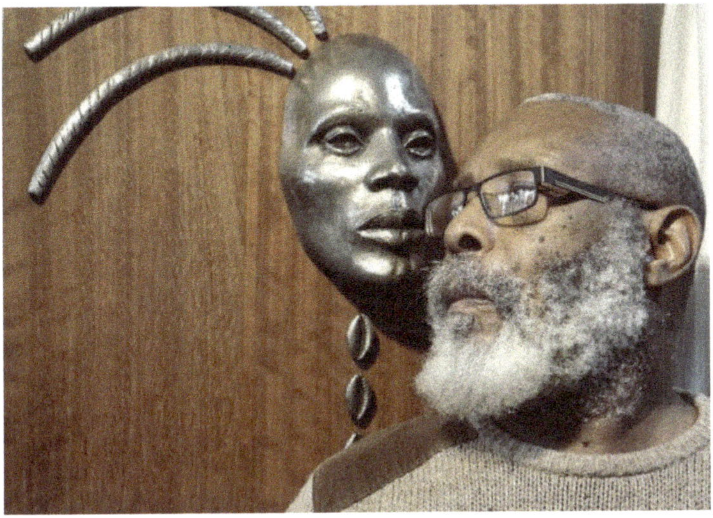

The Dancer's Mask

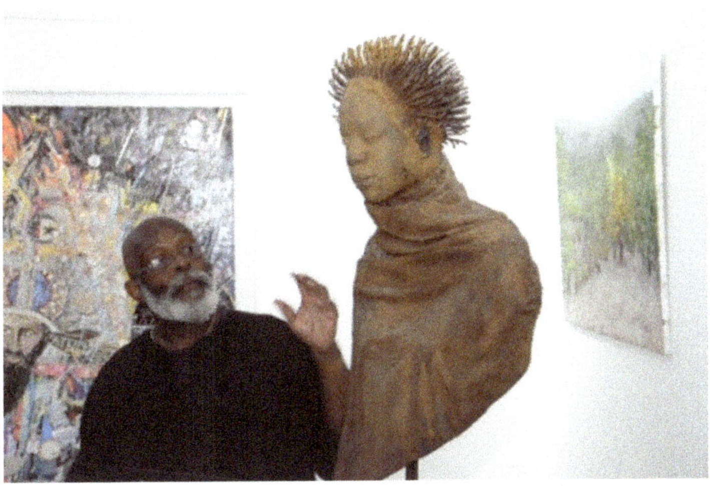

Meditations Beneath Duppy Cherry Tree: Sculpted from an original photograph captured by Hassan Aliyu

ABOUT THE AUTHOR

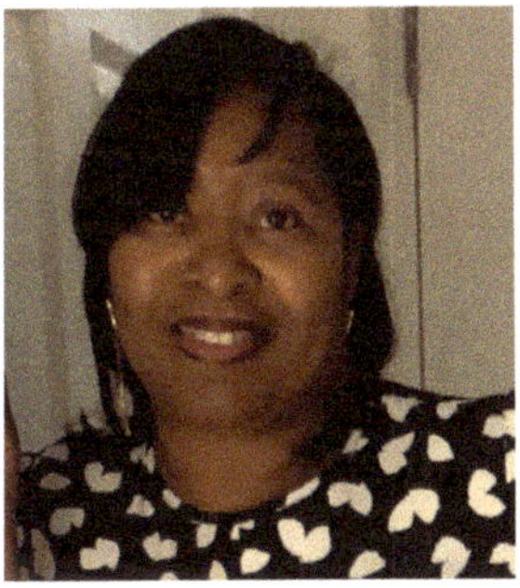

J.K. Andrews, an author and educator, was born in Lewisham, southeast London, to Lecietta and Peter Andrews, originally from Carriacou, West Indies. Joan is the youngest of five children. With her siblings, Leonard, Theresa, Ann and Margaret, she shares a rich family history that is rooted in the Caribbean. While her eldest siblings were born in Aruba, Margaret was born in Carriacou before the family migrated to England in the late 1950s, settling in the London borough of Lewisham.

J.K. Andrews began her writing career with the publication of her debut children's book, *The Brave Princess Shani*, in 1990. In addition to her literary achievements, she has dedicated decades to teaching, beginning her career in primary schools across Lewisham in 1987. From 2012 to 2018, she provided invaluable educational support to children receiving care, teaching in the schoolroom on the Children's Ward at Lewisham Hospital.

Currently, J.K. Andrews works as a supply teacher in the boroughs of Lewisham and Greenwich, continuing her lifelong passion for education and empowering young minds. Her work bridges a commitment to storytelling and teaching, reflecting her belief in the transformative power of creativity and learning.

www.ingramcontent.com/pod-product-compliance
Ingram Content Group UK Ltd.
Pitfield, Milton Keynes, MK11 3LW, UK
UKHW050650300425
5700UKWH00024B/172

9 781917 584401